THE VICTORY GARDEN KIDS' BOOK

Photographs by
Gary Mottau

Drawings by
George Ulrich

Design by
Alison Kennedy
WGBH Design

THE VICTORY GARDEN KIDS' BOOK

Marjorie Waters

Houghton Mifflin Company   Boston   1988

This book is an introduction to gardening for children. It is important that all learning experiences for children be properly supervised by attending adults, be they parents, family members, teachers, or friends. This is especially true where children will be learning to use unfamiliar tools and gardening materials, some of which may contain harmful chemicals or other additives. Please ensure that the children under your care are given the necessary level of supervision and guidance appropriate for their age, size, and level of ability, judgment, and maturity.

Library of Congress
Cataloging-in-Publication Data

Waters, Marjorie.
    The Victory garden kids' book/
Marjorie Waters; [photographs by
Gary Mottau : drawings by George
Ulrich].
        p.   cm.

    Includes index.
    1. Children's gardens.
2. Gardening. I. Mottau,
Gary.   II. Ulrich,
George.   III. Victory garden
(Television program)   IV. Title.

SB457.W34 1988   87-17194
CIP   AC
635—dc19

ISBN 0-395-42730-4
ISBN 0-395-46560-5 (pbk.)

Printed in the United States of
America

00 10 9 8 7 6 5 4 3 2 1

Photographs copyright © 1987 by
Gary Mottau, except photos on
pages 60 and 145 © 1987 by
Christopher Pullman and page 132
© 1987 by Ben Mottau

Drawings by George Ulrich

Design by
Alison Sommers Kennedy
WGBH Design
Boston, Massachusetts

Acknowledgments

All books are team efforts, but this one is really the shared offspring of many people who wanted to introduce kids to gardening. In particular, I would like to thank the creator of *The Victory Garden*, Russell Morash; the program's host, Bob Thomson, and producer, John Pelrine, for their time and support; Peter's Professional Plant Food and Potting Soil, Monrovia Nursery Company, and Mantis Manufacturing Company, the program's underwriters; and all the public television stations that make *The Victory Garden* possible. I would also like to thank the book's editor, Frances Tenenbaum, for her enthusiasm and guidance; Gary and Suzie Mottau, who so generously opened their house to an army of muddy feet every week; Nancy Lattanzio and Karen Johnson, of the Publishing Department of WGBH-TV, for their editorial direction and steadying hands through all the small crises; Chris Pullman, for his design direction, and Alison Kennedy, for designing such a beautiful and usable book; the University of Massachusetts Suburban Experiment Station and the Suffolk County (Massachusetts) Cooperative Extension Service for their cooperation; Julia McConnell, for her friendship, good spirit, and help; and my husband, Myles Gordon, for applauding in all the right places. And of course, I save the biggest thanks for John, Jenny, Joe, Julie, Sarah, Ben, and Sam, who made it an unforgettable summer in the garden.

*For Jim Crockett
who, at the age of three,
planted a bean
in a teacup.*

CONTENTS

PREFACE

Bob Thomson helping the kids close the garden in the fall.

Hi, kids, and welcome to the Victory Garden.

I've grown vegetables and flowers in my own garden for over fifty years and I hope to continue gardening for many more years.

You might be interested in my first garden. It wasn't much, I'm afraid, but it was a beginning. We lived in a house at the end of a road. There were lots of trees, and a brook ran along one edge of our property. In those days, back in the early 1930s, the country was going through some difficult times. It was hard for people to get jobs, and because people didn't have much money, they often lived with relatives, with a couple of families sharing the same house.

In my case, my mother and father and brother and myself shared a house with my grandmother and grandfather and one of my mother's elderly aunts. Back in those days, the men who had jobs worked every day except Sunday and the mothers and grandmothers seemed to be working all the time.

My grandfather, who had worked as a blacksmith, was retired, and his contribution to the family was to grow a fine garden. Working along with him as a youngster of three or four is my first recollection of working in a garden. As I look back over these many years, I realize that it was those very early attempts at planting and growing that ignited a spark of enthusiasm within me, which has burned brightly ever since.

As I've grown older, gotten married, and had children and grandchildren of my own, I've watched that same spark of enthusiasm rekindle in their lives. My wife, Betty, and I have three children, Scott, Kathy, and David. They're all grown up now, but they still live nearby and visit us often. About three years ago, our daughter Kathy and her husband had a little boy, named Todd. As soon as Todd could walk, he would follow me into the garden. Todd comes to see us often, perhaps three or four times each week. He has a set of tools that are just his size, and when I dig, Todd digs beside me, when I rake, he rakes, and when I plant, he plants, too.

Todd now knows the names of all the garden tools and what they are used for. We talk, he and I, about worms and birds and about frogs and toads, and we learn about having respect for the creatures that share the earth with us.

I couldn't have been more pleased when Marjorie Waters told me that she wanted to write a book that would help kids learn about gardening, and that Gary Mottau, who is a good friend of mine, would be photographing the kids in the garden at Holliston.

I think you will really like *The Victory Garden Kids' Book* and will learn many things from reading it. It's been fun for me to watch and listen to the kids whose pictures and stories are in this book. Perhaps your family and your friends and maybe even your grandfathers will be able to spend some time in your garden with you. I hope so, because I sure learned a lot from mine.

Bob Thomson

HOW TO GARDEN

KIDS IN THE VICTORY GARDEN

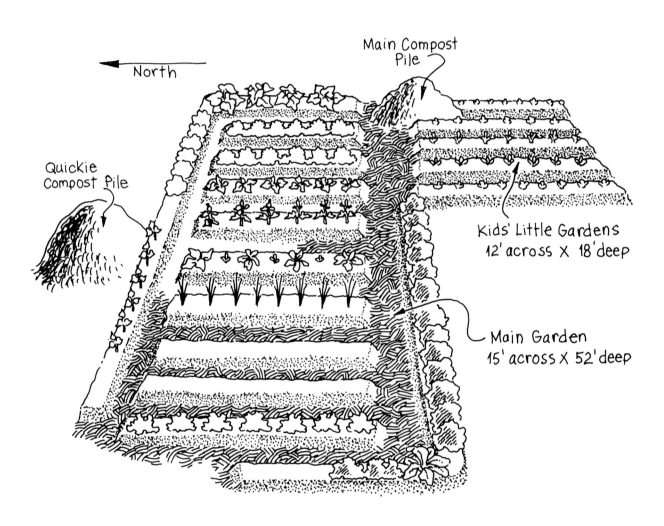

Main Compost Pile

North

Quickie Compost Pile

Kids' Little Gardens
12' across X 18' deep

Main Garden
15' across X 52' deep

The Kids' Victory Garden through the season. In May, there were only a few strawberry plants, and some lettuce seedlings that Ben is watering. In November, the garden is closed, and the winter rye is starting to show. In between, everything grew.

May

June

The Victory Garden Kids' Book is for kids starting their first garden or kids who have tried a little gardening before. It tells you everything you need to know about buying plants and using tools and planting seeds and watering crops and picking the harvest. It doesn't tell you how to eat what you pick, but you can probably figure that out on your own.

The book is a companion to *The Victory Garden*, a program on public television that's hosted by Bob Thomson. Every week you can watch Bob and other gardeners working in real gardens, and see what actually happens to the pumpkins and the petunias as they grow. You might want to watch the show while you're working on a garden of your own.

Like the television show, *The Victory Garden Kids' Book* traces a real garden through a whole season. But the gardeners in this book are kids, aged three to thirteen, and their back-yard victory garden is behind a big white house in Holliston, Massachusetts.

The book is based on what the kids learned and liked best in their first year of gardening. It's in two parts. This part, "How to Garden," will tell you where to start and how to do the big jobs of gardening. These jobs are the same no matter what you're planting. The chapters are in order, starting with the first steps you do in the spring and ending with what to do when you close the garden in the fall. These chapters are the most important part of the book. If you know how to do these big jobs, you can grow almost anything.

The second part, "Kids' Crops," starts on page 80 and tells you what you need to know about thirty different

July

August

November

What Makes It a Victory Garden?

The first victory gardens were just small back-yard vegetable gardens. During World War II, the government asked Americans to grow as much of their own food as they could, to free the farmers and food packagers and truckers to fight the war. Many of these people had never had a garden before, but they picked up a few tools and some seeds and gave it a try. They liked it so much that Americans have been gardening in their back yards ever since.

fruits, vegetables, and flowers that are all easy to grow.

The kids in the Kids' Victory Garden were all beginners in the garden. Some had tried a few gardening projects, but nobody had grown a garden from start to finish. They came because it sounded like fun. That's what really matters. If you're interested in gardening, you'll be able to do it, no matter how old you are.

There will be times when you'll need some help, but you can do almost everything yourself. Even in your first season you will learn a lot about gardening. Next year you'll learn more. For now, you don't need to know anything. Just use the book to grow the plants you want, and you'll have a little victory garden in no time.

John Dennison holding Christopher Mottau

Jenny Oliver

Joe Carney

Sarah O'Neill

Ben Mottau

Julie Evett

Sam Gordon

GETTING STARTED

You can start your garden in the spring, as soon as the soil is dry enough. Soil is the brown stuff your plants grow in. It's also called the ground, earth, the land, and dirt. It should be moist but not wet. After the winter ice and snow melt, you need to wait another month or so while the sun dries the soil a little. In our Victory Garden, the soil is usually dry enough in March or April, depending on how wet the winter and spring are. If it's warmer where you live, your soil might be ready in February.

The Kids' Victory Garden in the spring, dry enough for working. Some beds have been turned, others still have winter rye growing on them.

The soil at left has been squeezed and is so wet that the water oozed out. It's too early to work this soil. The soil at right passes the chocolate-cake test and is dry enough to plant.

There's a test to see if the soil's ready. Stand next to the garden — not right on it, because walking on wet soil is bad for the garden — and pick up a handful of soil. Squeeze it a little, so it makes a ball. Now flick your finger into it. If it stays in a clump, it needs more time to dry out. If it falls apart and looks like chocolate cake crumbs, it's ready.

Most gardeners are dying to get started in the spring, but you have to wait for the soil to be ready. Here are some things you can do in the meantime.

Pick Your Garden Spot

If you're using a garden that's been used before, you don't have to think about this. But if you're putting a new garden somewhere in your yard, you need to answer some questions first. Then you can use stakes or sticks to mark where your garden will go. The next chapter, "Digging," will tell you how to take off the grass and get the soil ready.

Where? You have to have sunshine for at least six hours a day to grow vegetables. Otherwise the seeds produce plants and leaves but not much fruit. If you don't have enough sunshine, try growing vegetables that have leaves that *are* food, like lettuce. Or try carrots, parsley, chives, or zucchini if you have only four or five hours of daily sun.

Once you have your spot, figure out which is the north side of the garden, because that's where tall plants should go, so they don't shade short ones. You can use a compass to find north, if you know how. Or you can stand facing the sunset. North is the direction to your right.

North →

Sunset

How to find north

Your garden needs to drain well. That means that the water sinks into the soil easily after a rain. Don't put your garden in a low spot in the yard where a puddle stays long after a rain.

Good soil is dark brown. But don't worry too much about what the soil looks like when you're picking a place for your garden, unless it's really rocky. You can almost always add things that will make it better.

How Big? Our Holliston garden for seven kids was much bigger than yours needs to be. You can get a big harvest from a garden that's only 4 by 4 feet. You probably don't want a garden bigger than 10 by 10 feet, because it would be too much work.

What Shape? This doesn't matter too much. Most people plant vegetables in rows, so their gardens are usually squares or rectangles. But your garden can be any shape you want.

Get a Soil Test

Soil is very complicated. There's a lot happening that you can't see but you need to know about. You find out by sending a little soil to a laboratory, which can test it and tell you what's in it.

The Yardstick Garden

All the chapters in "How to Garden" have a section called "The Yardstick Garden." This is a very easy kind of garden, and it's all planned for you. The book will tell you what to buy, exactly where to plant it, and how to pick what you grow. The Yardstick Garden is also small, just 3 feet square. You put it in a corner of a bigger garden, so most of the hard jobs get done when your family is working on the big garden.

There are only three crops in this garden: green beans, peppers, and zinnias. That's a nice mix of food and flowers. They all like warm weather, so you can start your Yardstick Garden when you know you won't have another spring frost. Read "Kids' Crops" to find out what you need to know about these three crops.

It's best to have your soil tested in the fall, but if this is your first garden, do it in the spring. You have to walk on the soil to collect samples to send to the lab, so give your soil time to dry out a little. And don't walk on it more than you have to.

The soil test will tell you two important things. One is how much lead is in your soil. Lead is a poison. It will get into your plants, and then into you. It's especially dangerous for kids, and you can't see it in the soil, which is why the soil test is so important for a kid's garden.

The test will also tell you whether your soil is acid, alkaline, or neutral. Sometimes acid soil is called *sour*, and alkaline soil, *sweet*. Your plants won't do well at all if your soil is either too sweet or too sour.

Finding a Lab You can buy soil-test kits in garden centers, but they won't tell you about lead. For that, you have to use a laboratory. You can ask about labs at your garden center, or call your local Cooperative Extension Service office. Its number is in the phone book, probably listed under county or state government. The agricultural extension agents are good people to know about because they answer all kinds of gardening questions over the phone.

Not all labs can test for lead, and some of the ones that can will charge a lot of money for it — $30 or more. Make sure the lab you use will check for lead, and ask how much they charge. If it costs a lot, the University of Massachusetts will do an inexpensive test for you, no matter what state you live in. The address is:

University of Massachusetts
Suburban Experiment Station
240 Beaver Street
Waltham, Massachusetts 02254

Just send a postcard to whichever lab you use, and ask for a soil-test kit. The kit will tell you how to collect your soil sample and where to send it. Then the lab will test your soil and mail you a report.

Too Much Lead?

The lab report on your soil test will tell you whether your lead level is low, medium, or high. If it's low, don't worry at all. If you have a medium level of lead, the report will tell you which plants you can grow. You should also be careful to wash your hands after you work in the garden, and wash your food before you eat it. If you have a high level, you shouldn't garden there, or play in the soil, or eat the food that grows there, especially if you're under six.

Lead comes mostly from peeling paint and car exhaust, so lead in the soil is worst near an old painted building or a busy street.

But farmers used to use an insecticide with lead in it, so lead can be a problem even out in the country. There's no way to get it out of the ground. But you can check other places in your yard to see if they're better. Or you can grow your garden in pots or window boxes, using soil you buy. See page 50.

Reading the Report The lab reports are some-times hard to read. Just look for two things:

- *How much lead is in your soil.*
  You probably won't find the word *lead*. The lab will use the scientific symbol, which is *Pb*. The lab will tell you how much lead is in your soil and whether that amount is dangerous.

- *How sweet or sour your soil is.*
  You can tell this by finding something called the pH number. Neutral soil has a pH of 7.0. If your soil is acid (sour), the pH number will be under 7. If your soil is alkaline (sweet), it will be over 7. The best pH for most vegetables is between 6.0 and 6.8, but almost all of them will grow if it's a little too high or too low. The lab will tell you if you need to fix your pH, which you do by adding either lime or sulfur when you dig your garden. (For more, see page 17.)

Keeping a notebook will help you remember important things about your garden.

Find Out Your Frost Dates

If you see a thin crust of white ice on a car or on the grass, that's frost. It means that the temperature has gotten cold enough for water to freeze. It doesn't matter whether the water is in a puddle or inside your plants, it turns to ice.

In most parts of the country, spring nights are cold enough for a frost. As you get closer to summer, there are

Cold-Weather Crops

Plant in spring, as soon as the soil is ready:
- chives
  leeks
- onions
- peas

Cool-Weather Crops

Plant about one week before your spring frost date:
  broccoli
  cabbage
- lettuce
- parsley
  radishes
- snapdragons

Warm-Weather Crops

Plant after the spring frost date:
- basil
- beans
  cantaloupe
  carrots
  cauliflower
  cucumbers
  eggplant
- impatiens
- marigolds
- peppers
- petunias
  potatoes
  pumpkins
  squash
  sunflowers
  tomatoes
  watermelon
- zinnias
  zucchini

- These are really easy crops.

no more nighttime frosts. People have been keeping records of frosts for years, so they know when different areas, even different towns, will probably have their last spring frost. This is called the last expected frost date or the spring frost date. In our Kids' Victory Garden, the spring frost date is May 10.

You need to know your spring frost date. You can ask your parents, or a neighbor who gardens. Your local garden center will probably know. Or you can call your local Cooperative Extension Service.

When you find out your spring frost date, you can get your fall frost date too. That's the date when the nights will again be cold enough for a frost. It's good to know both dates, because they tell you how long your garden will have warm weather. Our summer in the Kids' Victory Garden was about five months long. If you live in the South, it'll be much longer.

Frost is a funny thing. It can hit one garden and not hit another one very close to it. A garden that's out in an open field or in a low spot will have frost before one that has trees around it and is on a little hill. Keep that in mind when you find out your spring and fall frost dates.

Some plants don't mind frost at all. They are called cold-weather crops. Other crops will live through a frost, though it may slow their growth. These are the cool-weather crops. Warm-weather crops will die in a frost, so they do best in summer.

Order Tools

You won't like gardening much if you can't lift the tools. If you're a big kid, you can probably use regular adult tools. But if you're younger, you'll need special long-handled tools made for kids. In the Kids' Victory Garden, these tools made a big difference. Don't try using plastic toy tools. They'll break in ten minutes.

Kids' tools are hard to find. We finally found a set in a hardware store. They were called Little Giant, and were made by True Temper. They worked well, and didn't cost too much.

We also ordered a set through the mail. They cost a lot, but we thought they were better, especially for the

A group of kids' and adults' tools. On the left are shovels, and on the right are spades.

Spade

Iron Rake

Spading Fork

youngest kids. They had a handle that's easy to hold and were the right height. We bought them by catalogue from:

Smith and Hawken
25 Corte Madera
Mill Valley, California 94941

Both sets included an iron rake, a spade (a shovel with a sharp, squared-off blade), and a spading fork, which are the tools you really need. Both sets were well made of wood and metal.

If you take care of the tools, they'll last a long time. Make sure you put them away, under cover, when you're finished with them. As a safety measure, don't leave the iron rake or spading fork on the ground with the tines pointing up. If you step on the tines, the handle can pop up and bonk you in the head. It sounds like a strange accident, but it happened to us.

Looking at seed catalogues is a good idea even if you don't order your seeds by mail, because they're full of information.

Send for Catalogues

You can order garden catalogues through the mail. They come from seed houses, which are places that sell plants and seeds. They're full of information, and they're fun to look at while you're planning your garden. You can also order seeds through the mail.

To get a catalogue, just put your name and address on a postcard and say, "Please send your current catalogue." Send your postcard to one of these seed houses — or all of them, if you want.

The catalogues are free. And once the seed houses have your name, they'll send you new catalogues when they come out.

W. Atlee Burpee Co.
Warminster, PA 18974

Gurney's Seed
    and Nursery Co.
2nd & Capitol
Yankton, SD 57079

Harris Moran Seed Co.
3670 Buffalo Road
Rochester, NY 14624

Johnny's Selected Seeds
Albion, ME 04910

Otis Twilley Seed Co.
P.O. Box 65
Trevose, PA 19047

Stokes Seeds, Inc.
Box 548
Buffalo, NY 14240

Park Seed Co.
Hwy. 254 N.
Greenwood, SC
29647-0001

DIGGING

◄ Page 13. *John using a spading fork to turn over the winter rye in the spring. The rye decays and adds good food to the soil. It doesn't grow again and become a weed.*

Even after your soil is dry enough to pass the chocolate cake test, it will be heavy and matted down. You need to dig it and loosen it up. And you need to add things to the soil so it can feed your plants, just like you need to eat food to keep going.

This is the most important job you do in the garden. If you skip it, your plants may not grow at all. Or they may grow leaves but not make any fruit.

Digging takes some muscle, but all the kids at our garden liked it, because they had tools that were the right size for them and because we didn't do too much at once. The adults helped, too. You should do it the same way: work a little at a time, with the right tools and some help.

All this digging and adding is called soil preparation, which means getting the soil ready for planting. You do a little bit of soil preparation all season long, every time you plant. But you do the whole garden only twice, once in the spring and once in the fall. It's important to get this done early in the spring, even if you're too busy to plant any crops until school is out. Spend a Saturday morning on soil preparation, or you'll have a thriving weed patch by summer.

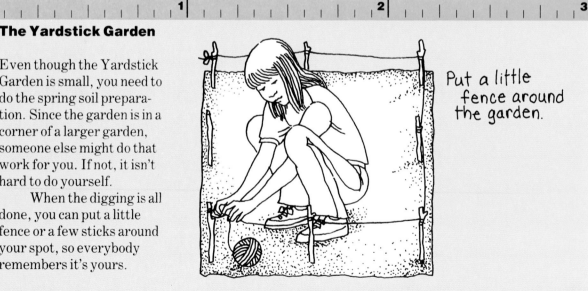

The Yardstick Garden

Even though the Yardstick Garden is small, you need to do the spring soil preparation. Since the garden is in a corner of a larger garden, someone else might do that work for you. If not, it isn't hard to do yourself.

When the digging is all done, you can put a little fence or a few sticks around your spot, so everybody remembers it's yours.

Put a little fence around the garden.

1 **Test the soil.** If you haven't had your soil tested yet, do it now. See page 7.

Removing Grass

Cut a square the size of your spade and lift up.

2 **Remove the grass or weeds.** If you're putting a garden where there wasn't one before, you have to remove the plants growing in the soil now, whether they are grass or weeds or whatever. You can't be sloppy about weeds and just yank the tops off the plants, because the roots will help the plants to grow back. You have to get the whole thing out, roots and all. Just do a little at a time. It's okay if it takes you a few days.

Grass will come off in sheets. Use your spade and slice down into the grass so you outline about a 5-inch square. Then work your spade under the square and pull it up. Keep going like this, slicing squares in the grass and lifting them up.

The top layer of soil, where the grass grows, is called topsoil, and it's the best soil in the garden. If you want, you can shake the topsoil off the roots, back into the garden. Or you can put the grass on the compost pile, if no weed-killer has been used on the lawn in the past year. The topsoil will end up back in the garden eventually. (The compost pile is the natural way to make food for your plants. See page 21.)

Removing Weeds

Push the spading fork in next to the weed and pull back on the handle.

Get the whole root out.

Removing weeds is easier, unless there are a lot of them. A spading fork works best, but you can use a spade or shovel. Push the tool down into the soil next to the weed, then pull back on the handle. This will pry the root out. Do your best to get the whole root. If you hear it break, you know there's some left behind, and you'd better dig some more. You might have to loosen big weeds in a couple of places. Put the weeds on the compost pile.

3 **Dig the soil.** The easiest and quickest way to dig the soil is to pay someone to come with a Rototiller, which is a machine that chops up the soil. Make sure you get the weeds out first. If the Rototiller turns them into the soil, they'll keep coming up all season.

Digging By Hand

Soil from first ditch.

First ditch was here.

Last ditch will be here.

If you have a small garden or some people to help, you can dig your garden by hand and pull the weeds at the same time. You have to dig deep, so your plants' roots will grow into soft soil. Dig at least as deep as the blade of your tool will go.

Here's how to dig by hand: Dig a ditch along one edge of the garden. Put the soil from the ditch into a wheelbarrow and take it to the other end of the garden. Now take little bites of soil off the side of the ditch, and turn them over into the bottom of the ditch. This will fill in the ditch and make a new one. If you keep filling in each new ditch, you'll turn all the soil in your garden. When you get to the end, use the soil in the barrow to fill the last ditch.

Soil is like soup. There's a lot in there that you don't notice when you're looking at the surface: old roots and leaves; little stones; tiny chips of minerals that shine like glass; bugs; worms; bacteria, too little to see, that make chemicals the plants need; rocks; broken glass; bits of plastic from a toy you left out three years ago; the flip top from a can of soda.

Take out the rocks, plastic, glass, and metal and throw them away. Be careful with anything sharp.

4 **Fix the pH.** The soil pH is the important information you get in your soil test. If the pH is right, the nutrients in the soil become dissolved in the water from the rain or your watering can. When the nutrients are dissolved, the plants can drink them in through their roots. If the pH is below 5.5 or above 7.5, the nutrients stay locked in the soil, and the plants go hungry.

It's easy to fix the pH. If your soil is too acid, add ground limestone, which is sometimes called lime. If your soil is too alkaline, add ground agricultural sulfur. Before you go to the garden center to buy lime or sulfur, measure your garden. Take the measurement and your soil report, and the people at the center will tell you how much lime or sulfur you need to correct the soil pH.

When you add lime or sulfur, sprinkle it evenly over the whole garden. It's easiest to use a coffee can to scoop it out of the bag. Don't spread lime or sulfur on a windy day, because it won't stay on the soil.

Worms are great for the garden because they wiggle around underground and make little tunnels that allow air and water into the soil. This keeps the soil loose, so the roots can grow easily.

5 **Add organic matter.** Organic matter is dead stuff that's decaying. It sounds awful, but it's not. When you walk in the woods, the earth under your feet is soft and springy because of all the dead leaves and pine needles. In nature, plants get their food from this decaying organic matter. The best organic matter for the garden is compost, because it's a mixture of plant and animal material. You can't buy it, but it's easy to make. Page 21 tells you how.

Manure is organic matter too. You can use manure from cows, horses, sheep, goats, chickens, or rabbits, but not from cats or dogs. When you use manure on the garden, it has to be at least one year old, and horse manure should be at least two years old. Fresh manure is too strong. You can buy manure from farmers or from people who have riding stables. If you have trouble finding some, the people at the garden center may be able to help.

Try to add both compost and manure to your garden. Spread them evenly on top of the soil in a layer no deeper than 3 inches.

Peat moss comes in big bags called bales. Just rip the bag open and use a spading fork or your hands to get it out.

Jenny using the back of an iron rake to prepare a raised bed. This makes it flat on top so it will drain well. That's the quickie compost pile behind her.

If this is your first garden, you probably don't have compost, and you may not be able to buy manure. So add a 3-inch layer of peat moss, which you can buy at a garden center. Peat moss doesn't actually feed plants, but it helps the soil absorb water, so plants can drink, even in hot weather. And buy a bag of blended organic fertilizer. The directions on the bag will tell you how much to add.

6 **Blend everything in.** You can probably do this with your spading fork. When you're finished, the soil will be so soft you can plant with your hands. That's just how it should be.

Raising the Beds

Beds are areas of soil that have been prepared for plants. Raised beds are just what they sound like — long hills with spaces in between, where you walk. Raised beds warm up earlier than flat beds in the spring, and dry out faster too, so you can get started earlier. Here's how you raise the beds:

Dig a path next to the garden fence. As you dig, put all the soil next to the path. Pretty soon you'll have a long mound of soil about 6 inches high. It should be about 3 feet wide.

Now flatten the top of the bed with the back of an iron rake. The top shouldn't slope off to one side, and it shouldn't have any high spots or low spots. The sides of the bed should be angled, not straight up.

Make a series of raised beds, leaving 12 to 18 inches between them so you can move around. Putting straw between the beds will help you see where to walk, and it will keep moisture in the soil.

Pile the soil next to the path.

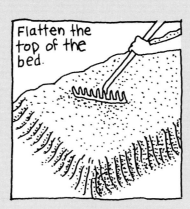

Flatten the top of the bed.

Put straw between beds.

7   **Rake the soil.** You need an iron rake for this. A leaf rake won't do the job. Rake the soil so it's smooth and level, with no hills or holes.

8   **Fence in the garden.** You probably need a fence to keep out animals. It doesn't have to be fancy, but it should be tall and strong. Chicken wire is okay, if it's 3 feet tall. You can buy it in hardware stores. You need 4-foot metal fence stakes too. And someone to help you put up the fence.

MAKING COMPOST

Starting a compost pile is like cooking dinner for your garden. The best food for soil is compost, which is plant and animal life that has decayed. You can't buy compost, but it's easy to make. Start as soon as you start your garden, and keep adding to it all season long.

Here are some of the things you can put in a compost pile:

- *Animal manure.* Cow manure (fresh or old) is best, but sheep, goat, chicken, and rabbit manure are also all right. Horse manure is okay if it's two or three years old.

- *Soil.* Every compost pile needs soil, because it contains the bacteria that make the compost happen.

- *Weeds and old plants* from the garden.

- *Grass clippings* from the lawn, as long as no weed-killer has been used on it in the last year.

- *Fruit and vegetable scraps* from the kitchen.

- *Leaves* that you rake in the fall.

Don't add meat, oily things, sweets, sticks, or diseased plants to your compost pile.

Opposite. *Ben taking a barrow full of garden weeds and plants to the compost pile.*

The Yardstick Garden

This garden is too small for you to make a good compost pile. But you can add to the one that goes with the big garden you're in. Just put the weeds you pull out, and later the plants (when they're finished growing), on the compost pile. You can also help add the limestone, manure, soil, and water.

Put pulled weeds on the compost pile.

The main compost pile, with two big zucchini plants growing together and some chives and petunias the kids planted. The watermelon will decay quickly because it's in small pieces.

To start a compost pile, follow these steps:

1 Find a place for it, either in the sun or in the shade. You need a spot about 6 feet square. When it's finished, the pile should be about 4 feet tall. Even a big pile like this will make only a little compost.

Put the pile inside the garden if you have room. That way it's easy to get to when you have weeds or old plants to add, and you can water it when you water the garden. You can also grow plants on top of the pile. We grew two zucchini plants on ours, and still kept adding to the pile all summer. (When we added anything, we put it on the sides of the pile, not right on top of the plants.) If you don't have room in your garden, put the compost nearby. Otherwise you'll forget about it.

2 Put some plant material together to get it started. You can use leaves, grass, and weeds from the garden. It's good to have some fresh green plant material, and some that's old and brown, like last year's leaves.

Organic matter decays faster if it's in small pieces. So chop up big, hard things, like old broccoli plants and watermelon rinds, into pieces the size of an apple. Even soft leaves are better chopped. In the Kids' Victory Garden we used a leaf shredder to make the leaves as small as snowflakes. If your family doesn't have a shredder, you can use whole leaves, but they'll take longer to decay. Or you can run over the leaves with a lawn mower to break them into pieces. You may need an adult's help.

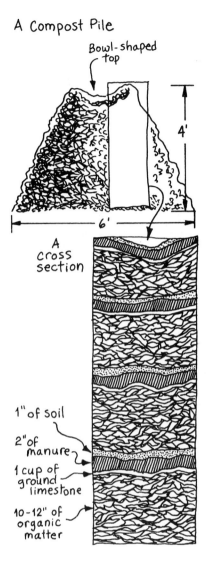

A Compost Pile

Bowl-shaped top

4'

6'

A cross section

1" of soil

2" of manure

1 cup of ground limestone

10-12" of organic matter

3 Compost piles are built in layers. When the bottom layer is 10 to 12 inches deep, sprinkle 1 cup of ground limestone evenly over the pile, to help everything decay faster. Next add a 1- or 2-inch layer of manure. Finally, add about 1 inch of soil and water the pile.

If manure is hard for you to get, sprinkle 2 cups of cottonseed meal evenly over the pile instead. You can buy it in garden centers. If you don't use either manure or cottonseed meal, the compost won't have all the different nutrients your plants need. And in a garden where no fertilizers are used, a balanced diet is important.

4 Add whatever you can, whenever you can. When you have another 10 inches of plant material, add limestone, manure or cottonseed meal, and soil. Make sure the pile gets watered every week or so.

Your pile will decay faster if you make sure the top is slightly bowl-shaped. This will hold water, which then filters all the way down through the pile.

5 When you close the garden in the fall, throw on all the old plants you pull out. The pile will decay faster if you turn it over before winter. Just shovel it all into a new pile, so what used to be on top is on the bottom. When you finish, water the pile well and let it sit. You can use it next spring.

Quickie Compost

If this is your first garden, you won't have any compost from last year. But you can start a quickie pile that will be ready to use this season. The secret is to put in things that are already partly decayed. Use old manure (or cottonseed meal), old leaves, soil, and limestone. Put the whole pile together at once in the spring, and don't add anything more to it. Make sure it's watered every week.

The compost pile will be ready to use by fall, but you can use some of it during the summer. We added a shovelful of quickie compost to the garden when we put in new crops. We also planted squashes, pumpkins, cantaloupes, and watermelons on top of it. By the middle of the summer it looked like a giant leafy animal asleep next to the garden. In the fall we dug the whole pile into the garden soil.

quickie compost pile

The garden in the middle of summer. The quickie compost pile is to the left of the garden, just outside the fence, and covered with plants.

BUYING WHAT YOU NEED

Garden centers are stores that sell seeds, plants, and supplies. Some are enormous, so before you go, make a list of what you want to buy. Then check the "Kids' Crops" section to see which plants you want to grow. Don't make the list too long. Four or five crops is plenty. Even one is plenty, if that's what you want.

"Kids' Crops" will tell you how much space a crop needs when it's full-grown, how long it will take to grow, and how much food you'll get from each plant. It will also tell you if a plant is an annual or perennial. Annuals are plants that grow for one season, then make seeds and die. Perennials live for several years, even through hard winters. You don't have to remember everything about the crops now. But you need to know, for instance, that a cherry tomato plant gets to be tall and grows hundreds of tomatoes, but a cabbage plant stays pretty short and grows only one head of cabbage.

Picking out just the plants you like is one of the best things about gardening. When the kids put in their gardens, they bought and planted what they wanted, and every one of the gardens was a little different. Sarah planted a bright red flower called a salvia. Joe picked a little mint plant because he liked to rub his hands over the leaves. Jenny loved all kinds of flowers, so she planted cosmos she had grown herself and snapdragons. Julie liked the dark green crinkly leaves of parsley. So if you like a plant you see at the garden center, ask about it and try it.

The Yardstick Garden

Here's what you need to buy for your Yardstick Garden:

Green bean seeds.
Make sure you see the words *bush* and *snap* on the package, or you won't be buying the right seeds. You'll need two packages.

Pepper seedlings.
Look at what your garden center has. Buy any variety that will be about 18 inches tall when it's full-grown. Check to see whether the variety is sweet, which means mild, or hot, which means it'll burn your tongue.

Zinnia seedlings.
Buy either a dwarf or a semidwarf variety. *Dwarf* means shorter than the regular varieties, which are 2 or 3 feet tall. The dwarf and semidwarf zinnias are all about a foot tall or less. These are easier because they stand up on their own, without staking. If the garden center doesn't have short zinnias, try a dwarf marigold.

Seeds

There will be a lot of choices on the seed rack — different kinds of tomatoes, different kinds of beans, different kinds of radishes. Most seeds are packed in paper envelopes that tell you the name of the variety of the plant. Each variety is a little bit different. For example, there are many different varieties of green beans, all with different names, like 'Tendercrop' and 'Greencrop.'

Some varieties are really better than others. If you see the words "All-America Winner," those seeds should do very well anywhere in the country.

Seed racks are fun to look at, and you can end up buying crops you don't need, or crops that it's too late to plant or that won't do well in your garden. Read the labels and check with the people in the garden center to see whether you've picked out good seeds.

The varieties we grew are listed in "Kids' Crops." You can buy the same ones if you want. Or you can try

Two packages of 'Crimson Giant' radish seeds, from different seed houses. The seeds inside are the same, though the packages are not.

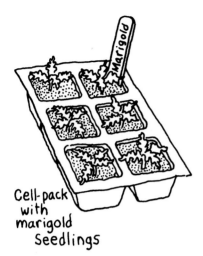

Cell-pack
with
marigold
Seedlings

Peat pot
with
squash
seedling

Flower
pot with tomato
seedling

Some of the seedlings and supplies bought at the garden center, and Sam, not quite sure what to do next.

another variety. You can also try some plant you never heard of. When we went to the garden center, Joe bought oriental radish seeds, just because they looked interesting. When he harvested them, he was pretty proud of himself, because nobody who worked on the garden — the kids or the adults — had ever grown or tasted them.

Seedlings

Seedlings are the fastest way to grow plants, and the easiest. Seedlings are young plants, about two months old, that have been grown from seeds. They cost more than a package of seeds, and you get only a few plants. But they are two months old already, so your crop is ready sooner. Anyway, you don't usually need all the plants you can grow from a package of seeds.

Garden centers sell seedlings (which they sometimes call transplants) mostly in the spring, so shop early. They grow seedlings only for plants that do well right in their area, so you know that the varieties for sale are good where you live.

Seedlings are most often sold in groups in one container. The best containers are cell-packs, which are little plastic cups joined together. Some cell-packs have 4 cups, some 6, some 8, some more. One plant grows in each cup.

Sometimes seedlings are sold in flats, which are like small rectangular cake pans. The problem with flats is that the roots of the plants get tangled up together. The cell-packs are better, because they keep each plant separate. You can tell whether you've got a flat or a cell-pack by looking underneath for the little cups.

Garden centers may sell some plants in single flowerpots. These are a good idea if you don't want many plants. Sometimes the containers are peat pots, which feel a little like cardboard. They're made out of peat moss, and when you plant, you plant the pot too.

There will probably be labels stuck in the soil that say what the plant is. Keep the labels with the plants so you remember which plants are which.

Supplies

You need only a few supplies. One is stakes to use as row markers when you plant. They look like big popsicle sticks, and usually they're made of wood.

If you're going to grow your own seedlings, you can buy containers like cell-packs. You can also buy a bag of potting soil. And you might want to buy a small bag of sand to use when you're planting small seeds. Page 37 tells you how to use the sand.

John, Joe, and Ben with a wagon full of seedlings. Those are petunias on the table behind them.

Picking the Best

When you're buying seedlings, pick the healthiest ones you can find. Here's what to look for:

Short growth.
The plant shouldn't tower over the container.

A lot of leaves.
The leaves should be close together on the stem.

Good color.
Most seedlings should have healthy-looking green leaves.

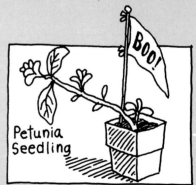

Good posture.
The seedlings should stand up straight, with crisp-looking leaves.

Growing Your Own

You can grow your own seedlings in the spring if you have a place indoors that's sunny most of the day. (If you don't have enough sun, buy your seedlings.) All you do is plant seeds in pots of soil. Later you move the seedlings to the garden. The "Kids' Crops" section tells you whether starting your own seedlings is a good idea. In the Kids' Victory Garden, Jenny started her own flower seedlings, and they grew and bloomed all summer long.

When you start the seeds is important. Check "Kids' Crops" to find out when the seedlings can go in the garden. Plant the seeds four or five weeks earlier.

Here's how to grow your own:

1 Start with clean containers that have holes in the bottom or that are made of some material that will let water seep through. You can buy small flowerpots or cell-packs or peat pots. Or you can use a cardboard egg carton, or a plastic one if you punch little holes in the bottom of the sections so water drains out.

2 Fill the containers almost full with sterile potting soil that you buy. (Don't use soil from the garden, because it may contain insects, weeds, or diseases that will harm the seedlings.) Press the soil down a little as you put it in.

3 Put one seed in each container. (If you don't mind thinning later, put in two.) Plant some extra seeds. There are usually a few that won't sprout.

4 Cover the seeds with a little soil, just enough so you can't see them anymore. Pat the soil with your fingers.

5 With a pencil or waterproof marking pen, write the name and variety of the plant on a stake or a popsicle stick. Put it into the soil at the edge of the container.

One week after the kids planted seeds in containers, the seedlings are up. Some plants grow more quickly than others, so some seedlings are bigger.

6 Water the soil by setting the containers in a pan of shallow warm water. Be sure the water is not deep enough to come over the tops of the containers. The water will seep up from the bottom. When the soil looks moist, take the containers out of the water. Put them on a cookie sheet and set them on top of the refrigerator, where the motor will keep them warm.

7 Seeds die if they dry out while they're sprouting. Spray them with water often enough to keep the soil moist. You can buy plant sprayers, which are sometimes called misters because they spray a mist. Or you can use an empty bottle of spray cleaner, but get every part of it good and clean first.

8 In a week or two, when you see little green specks on the soil, put the containers in a sunny place indoors, and keep the plants watered.

9 When the seedlings are about 4 inches tall, start getting them used to being outdoors. When it's not too cold or windy, put them outside during the day in a partly shady place. Full sunlight is too much for them at first. At night put them on

a porch, or someplace where they're covered but still outside. After a week of doing this, you can plant them in the garden.

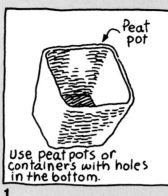

Peat pot

Use peat pots or containers with holes in the bottom.

1

Press the soil as you put it in the pot.

2

Pumpkin seed

Put one seed in each container.

3

Cover the seed with soil.

Pat the soil down.

4

Write the name of the plant on a stick.

Pumpkin

5

Set the container in a shallow pan of warm water.

6

Spray with water often.

Pumpkin

7

PLANTING SEEDS

To plant seeds outdoors, all you do is make a line in the soil, drop the seeds in, cover them up, and water them. Here it is, step by step:

1 Wait for a day when the soil is pretty dry. If the soil is really damp, it gets all over your fingers, and the seeds stick to your hands.

2 Get what you need:

- an iron rake
- the seeds
- stakes
- a pencil or waterproof marking pen
- a watering can with water in it

3 Figure out where you're putting your crops. Very tall plants, like sunflowers, belong by the north fence, so they don't shade shorter plants.

The Yardstick Garden

The only seeds in your Yardstick Garden are the beans. First mark out where they're going. Use your finger to draw a rectangle at the edge of your garden, 4 inches wide and 3 feet long.

Open the seed package and sprinkle the seeds into your hand. Then lay them about 2 inches apart on the rectangle.

Now poke each seed an inch or so into the soil. Cover the holes with soil so you can't see the seeds anymore. When you finish, water the soil.

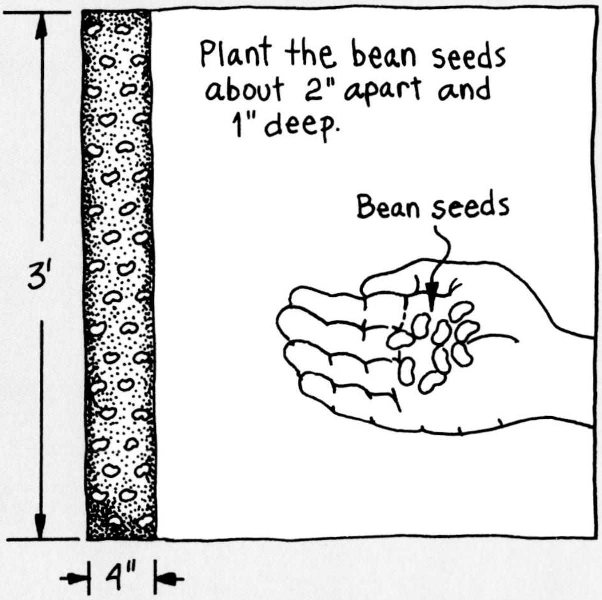

Plant the bean seeds about 2" apart and 1" deep.

Bean seeds

3'

4"

Rake the soil flat.

4

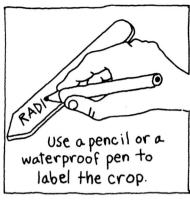

Use a pencil or a waterproof pen to label the crop.

5

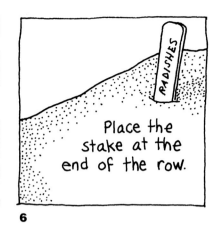

RADISHES

Place the stake at the end of the row.

6

4 Rake the soil with an iron rake, so it's flat, with no slants or bumps or holes. This allows the water to seep down to the roots.

5 Write the name of your crop on a stake. Use a pencil or waterproof marking pen. The ink from felt-tip markers runs when it gets wet.

6 Put the stake in the ground at one end of the row.

7 Starting at the stake, make a furrow — a shallow line — in the soil with your finger. Try to line it up straight with the row next to it. "Kids' Crops" will help you decide how long the furrow should be.

8 Open the seed packages. Just rip a corner so the seeds don't all spill out. Sprinkle a few seeds into your hand.

9 Put the seeds in the furrow, about half an inch apart. Some seeds are big and easy to plant, like cucumbers, peas, green beans, cantaloupe, squash, pumpkins, and zucchini. Some seeds are small but easy to handle because they're round, like radishes, broccoli, cabbage,

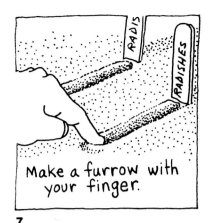

Make a furrow with your finger.

7

Sprinkle a few seeds in your hand.

8

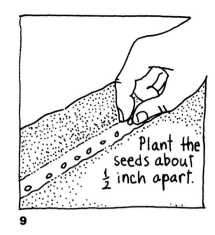

Plant the seeds about ½ inch apart.

9

It's good to have a handy "ruler" with you when you plant. Measure your thumb and each of your fingers, and the tips of your fingers to the first joint. Look for ½ inch, 1 inch, and 2 inches, which are the usual planting distances for seeds.

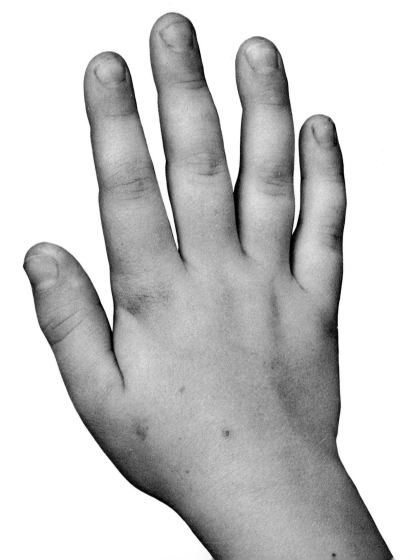

Jenny squeezing a furrow shut while John and Marjorie pat the soil so the sweet basil seeds are snug.

and cauliflower. Just pick up one seed at a time and put it in the furrow half an inch away from the next seed.

Small seeds, like carrots, lettuces, and many of the flower seeds, are hard to pick up one at a time. Take a little pinch of seeds between your thumb and index finger. Move your hand along over the furrow and rub your thumb and finger together. The seeds will fall out, and they'll be as far apart as you can get them.

How big the seeds actually are.

Green bean   Pea   Radish   Lettuce   Carrot

Squeeze the furrow closed.

10

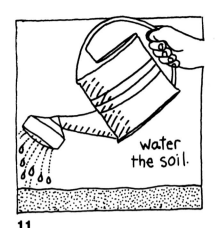

water the soil.

11

10 When the seeds are all in the furrow, squeeze it closed with your thumb and finger. Then pat the soil so the seeds are snug and covered.

11 Water the soil right after you plant the seeds. Don't just dump on a big pot of water — that would flood the seeds. Use a watering can with an attachment on the spout called a rose. This makes the water come out in a shower.

Making It Easier

There are some tricks you can use to make small seeds easier to plant.

Add a pinch of sand to a pinch of seeds. You can buy sand in garden centers. It gives your fingers more to hold, and the seeds go into the furrow farther apart.

If you order from a catalogue, you can buy seed tapes for some kinds of seeds. These are paper tapes that have the seeds stuck to them. You just lay the tape on the ground, cover it with a little soil, and water the row. The seeds are spaced evenly, which makes thinning easier later.

Or you can do what Sam did when he was planting carrots — forget about sowing in rows. Put some seeds in your hands and rub your hands over a small area of soil. Cover the seeds with soil and water them. The plants will come up, and you might not have to thin too much. (But you may have more trouble with weeds.)

Lay the seed tape on the ground and cover it with a little soil.

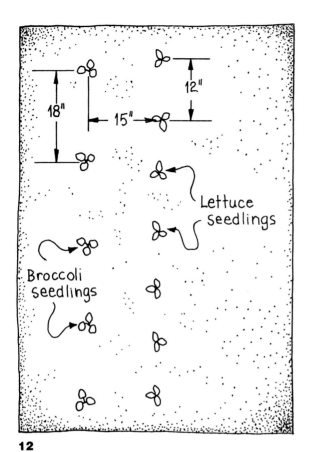

18"

12"

15"

Lettuce
seedlings

Broccoli
seedlings

12

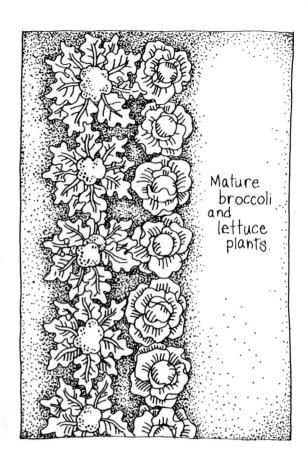

Mature
broccoli
and
lettuce
plants.

12 If you're planting another crop, you need to figure out how far apart your rows should be. You have to do some math, but it's not hard. Find out how wide your plants will get. "Kids' Crops" tells you this. Take the width of the two crops you're putting next to each other, add them together, and divide by 2. That's how far apart the rows should be. If you want a path between the rows, add another 10 inches or so.

Let's say you're putting lettuce in one row. Lettuce is 12 inches around when it's grown. Next to it you're putting a row of broccoli plants, which are 18 inches wide when they're grown. Add the two together: that's 30. Now divide by 2: that's 15. There should be 15 inches between the rows, or about 25 inches if you want a path.

13 When you're finished in the garden for the day, get out the hose and sprinkler and water the whole thing for 15 minutes. (If you want to know more

Sam planting bean seeds in his little garden. These seeds are planted in a path, not a furrow.

about watering cans and hoses and sprinklers, turn to page 53.) And every day until the seeds sprout, make sure the soil is moist — but not flooded!

Most seeds will sprout in a week or two. If you look closely, you will see tiny green specks on the soil. Usually you see the stem first, bent over, because it's trying to pull the first leaves up out of the ground. It will probably shine a little. It's a wonderful thing to see.

Once your seeds sprout, all you have to do is keep them watered during dry weather and thin them when it's time. To learn how to do this, see pages 53 and 56.

How the Seeds Grow

In moist soil, the outside of the seed cracks open. Tiny roots come out through the cracks and reach down into the soil. As the roots go down, two little leaves, called the seed leaves because they've been inside the seed, poke up and aim toward the light.

The seed leaves of most plants are plain and round. They don't look like the leaves of a tomato plant or a zucchini plant or a snapdragon. But the rest of the plant's leaves do. They're called true leaves.

All green plants reach for the sun, because the sunlight helps them use the food and water in the soil to make carbohydrates, which they need to grow. This process is called photosynthesis. You can't see it happening, but it's the reason that plants make food you can eat. And it's why your garden needs a place in the sun.

Green bean seedlings just coming up. They grow at different rates, so some have true leaves already, and some are just pulling their seed leaves out of the ground.

true leaves   seed leaves

PLANTING SEEDLINGS

◀ Page 41. *Joe planting 'Dark Opal' basil seedlings in his little garden. The red flowers are called celosia.*

Planting seedlings is easy, and it's a good way to start a garden, mostly because seedlings don't need to be thinned. You just put in the number of plants you want.

If you grew seedlings of your own in cell-packs, they're ready for the garden when they're 3 to 6 inches tall. But if you used an egg carton or some other container with small cups of soil, you need to transplant the seedlings — move them into the garden — before they're 2 inches tall. That's so the roots don't grow too big for the container.

The seedlings at the garden center will be ready to plant when you buy them, and you should plant them right away. They need to get into the soil so their roots can spread out. If you can't plant them right away, or if the weather isn't right yet, make sure you water them every day — even twice a day in hot weather.

To plant your seedlings, take them out of their containers, make a hole for them in the ground, put them in, and pull the soil around. Here it is, step by step:

Julie watering a table of seedlings before transplanting to the garden. Holding the sprinkler up high makes the water come down gently so the plants aren't hurt.

1 Water the seedlings in their containers. Water the garden too, if it's very dry. Seedlings are easier to plant in moist soil.

2 Get the soil ready. If you're planting the first crop of the season, you don't need to add anything to the soil. But if you've grown one crop in this soil already, work in some compost or old manure. That puts back some of the food the first crop used. Then rake the bed smooth with an iron rake, so there are no bumps or holes and no slants.

3 Decide where your plants are going in the garden. The tallest plants belong by the north fence, so they don't shade other crops.

The Yardstick Garden

First mark the spots where your seedlings go. Start by putting a yardstick across the top of the garden. At the 15-inch mark and the 30-inch mark, draw two lines down the soil. These are the lines for the peppers and zinnias.

Plant the two peppers first. Put the yardstick next to the pepper line, and poke your finger into the soil next to the 9-inch mark and next to the 27-inch mark. Use your hands or a trowel to make the poke holes bigger, and put one pepper plant in each. Give each one a cutworm collar, like the ones described on page 62. Make a fort of soil around each seedling, and fill the fort with manure tea or fish emulsion mixed with water.

Now plant the zinnias. Lay the yardstick next to the zinnia line and poke your finger into the soil at the 6-inch mark, the 18-inch mark, and the 30-inch mark. Make the poke holes bigger and put one zinnia in each hole. Make a fort of soil around each one, and fill the forts with water.

When you're finished, the whole garden should be watered. If adults are working in the big garden, this may be done for you.

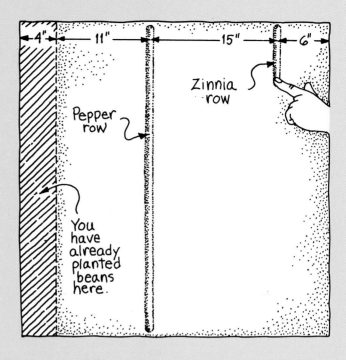

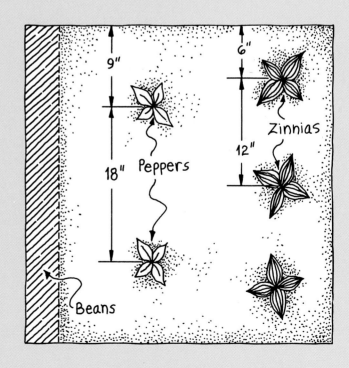

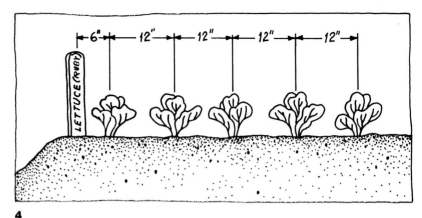

4

John planting 'Ruby,' 'Salad Bowl,' and 'Oak Leaf' lettuce seedlings.

4 Figure out where the plants are going to go in the bed. Do this by checking "Kids' Crops" to see how wide the full-grown plants are. If they're 12 inches wide, put them in 12 inches apart.

5 Mark the spots where your plants are going. In the Kids' Victory Garden we did this by poking one finger down in the soil, which leaves a hole you can see. If you measure the whole row and make your poke holes all at one time, you don't have to keep measuring every time you plant a seedling.

6 Make a planting hole at the first poke hole. Make it a little bigger than the root ball of your seedlings. (The root ball is the clump of soil and roots.) If your soil is as soft as it should be, you can use your hands. Or you can use a trowel, which is the gardening tool for making planting holes. We had several trowels at the Kids' Victory Garden, and the kids liked using them. But they used their hands more often.

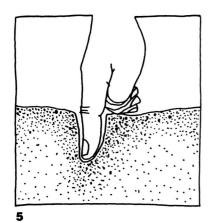

5

6

You can use your hand to measure planting distances for seedlings, too. Stretch your hand wide and measure from the tip of your thumb to the tip of your little finger. If it's about 6 inches, you can use one hand-span for seedlings that are 6 inches apart, two hand-spans for seedlings that are 12 inches apart, and so on.

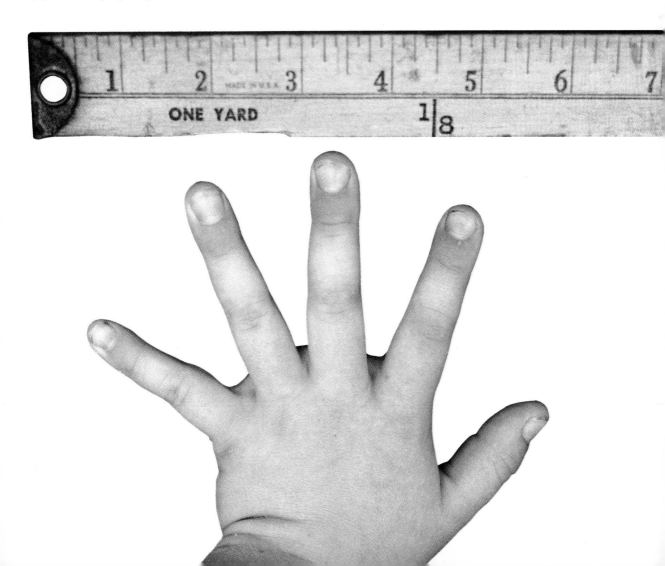

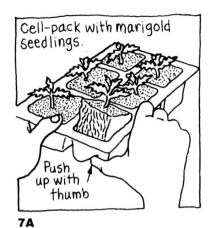

Cell-pack with marigold seedlings.

Push up with thumb

7A

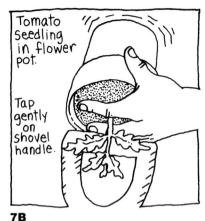

Tomato seedling in flower pot.

Tap gently on shovel handle.

7B

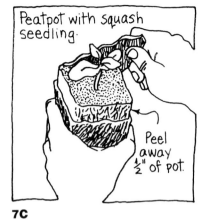

Peatpot with squash seedling.

Peel away ½" of pot.

7C

7 Now take one seedling out of its container. Don't yank it out, or the stem or roots might break. Hold the stem gently and push up a little from the bottom of the container.

If your plants are in egg cartons, you can do the same thing, but the bottoms of the cartons might not give as easily as cell-packs do.

If your plants are in separate flowerpots, put two fingers gently around the stem at the bottom of the plant. Turn the pot upside down and tap the rim lightly on a table. Or stick a shovel in the ground, turn the pot upside down, and tap it lightly against the handle. The plant should come right out in your hand.

Trowels

A good trowel should be made of one piece of metal, so there's no place for it to break. You can also use strong aluminum flour scoops. Don't try to use a regular kitchen spoon for planting — it might bend like a pretzel the first time you try!

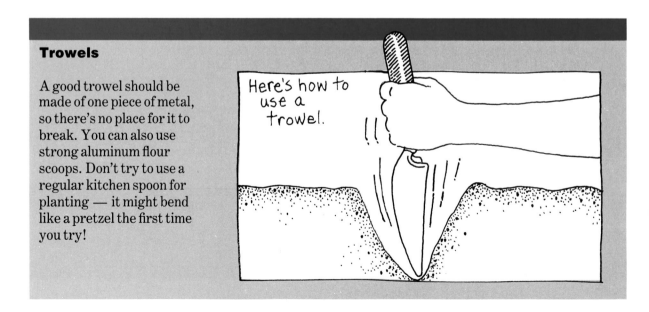

Here's how to use a trowel.

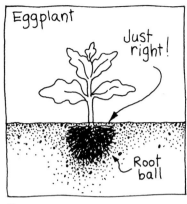

8

If your plants are in peat pots, you don't need to take them out at all. Just plant the pot too. But peel the top of the pot back so it doesn't stick up above the soil and draw water away from the plant.

8 Set the plant into the first planting hole. Hold it so that the soil around the seedling is even with the garden soil. The plant shouldn't be too low or too high. Pull soil around the roots, and press the soil gently so there are no empty spaces near the roots. When the plant is in the ground, smooth the soil all around so there are no bumps or holes.

Jenny laying out her cosmos seedlings in the right places in her little garden. There were cucumber seeds in the cage to the left.

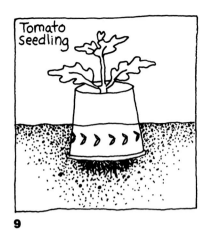

Tomato seedling

Manure tea

9

10

11

9 Cutworms attack the stems of little plants. If your crop needs cutworm collars to protect it ("Kids' Crops" will tell you this), put one collar around each seedling and press it about 1 inch into the soil. You can buy these collars, or make your own. See page 62.

10 Use your hands to pull soil in a circle around the outside of the plant, or the cutworm collar if you are using one. You should end up with a fort around the plant, about 2 inches tall. When you water, the fort will keep the water around the stem so it goes down to the roots.

11 Feed your seedlings. In the Kids' Victory Garden we used manure tea (see page 53). If you can't get any manure, you can buy liquid fish emulsion from a garden center and mix it with water in your watering can. Water each new plant with this by filling in the fort once, letting the water soak in, and filling it again.

12 Mark the rows by writing the name and variety of the crop on a stake. Write the date you planted too, if you want. Use a pencil or waterproof marking pen. The ink from most felt-tip pens runs when it's wet.

Write the name of the plant and the date on the stake.

12

13 If you're planting another crop, you need to figure out how far apart your rows should be. Check "Kids' Crops" to find out how wide your plants will get. Take the width of the two crops you're putting next to each other, add them together, and divide by 2. That's how far apart the rows should be. Add 10 inches for a walking path. (For more about this, see page 38.)

14 When you're finished in the garden for the day, get out the hose and sprinkler and water the whole garden. If you need to know more about how to do this, see page 55.

Pots and Window Boxes

You can grow plants in great big containers and keep them on a porch or balcony all season long. In the Kids' Victory Garden we used big wooden flowerpots that were really wine barrels cut in half. You can get them from a lumberyard or garden center. We also used old cement pots. It doesn't matter what you use, as long as it's big. Here are the steps:

1 Your containers need holes in the bottom so water can drain out. If the container is made of wood, you can drill holes in it. We did this to the wine barrels. (If you have to drill them, make sure there's an adult with you.) If you buy pots, they'll probably have drainage holes already.

2 Fill the container with a mix of garden soil, potting soil (which you buy at a garden center), and compost in equal amounts.

If you don't have an outdoor garden and can't get compost or garden soil, use potting soil.

3 Use your hands or a trowel to make a hole, and put the plant in. Close up the hole around the roots. Follow the advice in Step 8 in "Planting Seedlings," page 47.

4 Water the soil, using a watering can with a rose (see page 54). You need a lot of water, but don't add it all at once. Pour some on, let it sink in, and pour more on. When you see water coming out the bottom, you can stop.

5 Keep the soil moist, but not sopping wet, all season long. Soil in containers dries out quickly. You may have to water every day. Once a week, feed the plants with manure tea or fish emulsion. (Container-grown plants need to eat very well.)

One of the wine-barrel gardens, crammed full of silvery dusty miller, one tall cleome about to flower, some lavender lobelia in the front of the container, and two purple sweet alyssum flowers to the right.

TAKING CARE OF
THE GARDEN

◀ Page 51. *Julie trying to catch some water from the sprinkler, and maybe take a little shower on a very hot day. The plants are part of Gary's perennial garden.*

Plants need to be taken care of, just like pets. If nobody does this, the garden will turn into a big mess, and there won't be much to pick.

The best thing is to visit your garden every day or so and see how things are going. Is the soil dry? Is there a plant that's wilting? Are there weeds growing right in the middle of your radishes?

Look for the good things too. On one of our trips through the Kids' Victory Garden, Sarah lifted up a pumpkin leaf and found our first green pumpkin. This was a big treat. It's always hard to believe your plants will really do this. Even adults who've been gardening a long time are a little surprised every year.

These are the main things you do to take care of your garden: feeding, watering, thinning, weeding, and, for some plants, caging or staking to help them stand up straight.

Feeding

If you're putting a good amount of organic matter, like compost or manure, on your garden, your plants will be eating well. But they still like some extra snacks while they grow. In the Kids' Victory Garden we used manure tea for this, but some people use liquid fish emulsion from a garden center instead. Just follow the directions on the bottle, and be careful not to get it in your eyes or on your skin.

The Yardstick Garden

This garden doesn't need much work. There's nothing to thin. You will have to weed, but the garden is so small that it won't take long.

But do remember to keep the bean seeds watered while they're sprouting. If your Yardstick Garden is watered when the big garden is, you don't have to worry about the weekly watering. Feed your plants every two or three weeks with manure tea or fish emulsion, though.

Feed seedlings right after you plant them. Just fill up the fort of soil once, let the water sink in, and fill it again. Every two or three weeks while they grow, feed the crops again. If you plant seeds right in the garden, wait until you thin the plants, and then start feeding them every two or three weeks.

Keep an eye on your crops. If you see yellow leaves, the plants are hungry, and you should feed them right away.

Watering

Plants drink water from the soil. All plants need water the whole time they're growing. You have to water new crops after you plant them. And every week you should water the whole garden, if there hasn't been 1 inch of rainfall during the week.

Manure Tea

Manure tea is water that has had manure soaking in it. It sounds pretty terrible, but one of the kids at the Kids' Victory Garden once rinsed his hands in it without looking, and he never knew the difference.

Here's the recipe: Take a 5-gallon bucket and put in a shovelful of year-old manure from cows, horses, sheep, rabbits, goats, or chickens. Then fill the bucket with water and let it sit for a couple of hours. When you need the tea, scoop some into a coffee can and pour it onto your plants. Don't use your watering can with a rose. It'll get all clogged up.

As you use the tea, you can keep adding water and making more. After a while, when it gets moldy and a little green, dump it on the compost pile and start again.

Measuring the Rain

It's hard to know how much water falls during a rain unless you use a rain gauge. Here's an easy one to make.

Take a heavy wide-mouthed glass jar, like a peanut butter jar. Push it into the soil a little so it won't tip over. When it rains, the jar will catch the water. Once a week, pick the jar up and measure the water with a ruler. If there hasn't been 1 inch of rain, get out the hose and sprinkler. Make sure you empty the jar once a week, or after a rain or a watering.

If you have a hot, sunny day, some of the water will evaporate if you don't cover the jar.

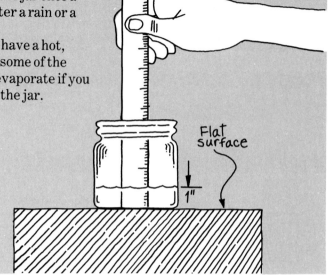

Flat surface

1"

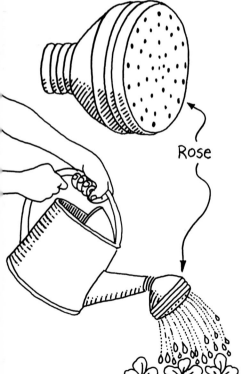

Rose

Right After Planting Water seeds and seedlings as soon as they're in the ground. This is called watering in. You do this with a watering can. If you use a big watering can, fill it partway so it isn't too heavy. At the Kids' Victory Garden, the youngest kids used a houseplant watering can, which is small and easy to lift. Either size should have a special piece on the spout called a rose, which makes the water come out in a gentle shower.

The best way to water newly planted seeds is to stand over the row and move the can back and forth while the water comes out, so you don't water the same spot for too long. Stop if you see puddles on the soil. Let the water sink in and then water the row again.

You may have to water your seeds every day while they're sprouting, and even twice a day in hot, sunny weather. Raised beds dry out faster than flat rows. Remember, if the seeds dry out, the crop is gone.

Seedlings should be watered in too. In the Kids' Victory Garden we used manure tea and fed them at the same time. You can use fish emulsion or just water. Whatever you use, fill the fort of soil you made around each seedling. Pour the liquid gently so you won't hurt the plant if you hit it and you won't wash the soil away from the roots.

The Whole Garden You can't water just the rows where the seeds and seedlings are, because dry soil nearby will draw the moisture away from your plants. You have to make sure the whole garden gets watered with a hose and sprinkler. This is really important in hot weather, when things dry out very fast.

How do you know whether the soil needs water? For one thing, dry soil is light in color, and moist soil is dark. If the soil is very dry, it looks dusty. You can also tell by poking your finger an inch or so down into the soil. If it feels dry, it's time to water.

A garden needs 1 inch of water a week, either from rain or from you. You can water the soil if it looks or feels dry. Or you can make a rain gauge.

Try to remember how often it rains. If you have a long rainy day, you probably won't need to water for another week. But you should check the soil to be sure.

The whole garden being watered on a bright, hot day. The sprinkler is set up on a trash can so the force of the spray doesn't hurt the nearby plants.

Thinning

When you plant seeds in a row, the plants often grow too close together. They have to be thinned. That means you have to pull some out and give the others room to grow.

We didn't always do a good job of this in the Kids' Victory Garden. We let one row of carrots go, and we had a real tangle in there. We did weed it finally, but when we picked the carrots, most of them were really puny and only partly orange.

Here's how you thin a row:

1 Wait for the plants to grow to about 2 inches tall. If you thin after a rain or after watering, the plants will come out easily.

2 Check "Kids' Crops" to see how far apart your seedlings should be when you're finished thinning. For example, carrots need to be 2 inches apart. That means saving one seedling every 2 inches and pulling out all the ones in between. Have something with you to measure with — either part of your hand that's the right length, or a ruler.

Radish seedlings, next to pink petunias, needing thinning right away. Try to picture a whole radish growing under each seedling, and you'll realize how crowded they are.

Leave one seedling every two inches.

3 Start at one end of the row. Save the first big seedling. Then go down the right number of inches and figure out which seedling you're going to save next. Pull out the seedlings in between. Keep going down the row like this. If your seedlings are growing really close together, put your fingers around the stem of the plant you want to save and pull the ones that are nearby. That will hold the good plant in the soil.

4 Some seeds, like pumpkins, are planted in groups. When they sprout, they need thinning too. Save the two that are the biggest and healthiest and pull the others out. Put the pulled seedlings on the compost pile.

Weeding

Weeds are plants you don't want, growing where you don't want them. They take up space and attract bugs and get tangled up with your plants' roots.

One way to keep weeds out—and moisture in—is with a mulch, which is a cover for the soil. Use wood bark, straw, or salt-marsh hay, all of which you can buy in garden centers. Or use dry grass clippings if no weed-killer has been used on the lawn during the past year. Spread the mulch over the soil a couple of inches thick.

Is It a Weed?

When your crops are little, it's sometimes hard to know which green things are the weeds. The first thing to do is figure out which plants are your crop. They will be in a row (if you put your seeds in a row). And they'll look alike. They'll be about the same size and have the same kind of leaves. Everything else is a weed. One of the weeds you'll see most is grass. If you pull out a good plant by mistake, try putting it back in the ground. It may grow.

Julie holding a crabgrass weed she pulled out, big root and all.

Jenny using a magic weeder to weed her little garden and loosen the soil so the water seeps down to the roots easily.

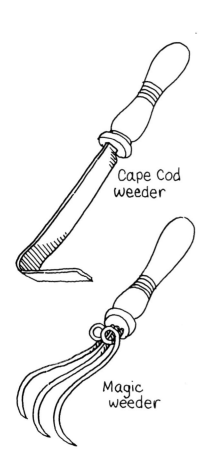

Cape Cod weeder

Magic weeder

Even if you use a mulch, a few weeds will sneak into your garden. You need to get rid of them. The best thing is to do a little weeding every week, even if the weeds aren't very big. You can use stand-up tools, like hoes, but it's easier to get down on your knees and use a hand tool. The best ones are a three-pronged cultivator, called a magic weeder, and a Cape Cod weeder.

Be careful with these tools — they're sharp. But they're easy to use. Just comb lightly through the top of the soil around your plants. Don't go close enough to hurt them. The tool will break little weeds so they can't grow very much. It also makes the soil loose, which lets water and air get down to the roots.

You may still have weeds that grow pretty big. You have to pull them out. The trick is to get the whole root. Little pieces of root left in the soil will grow new weeds. If the weed is very close to one of your plants, hold the good plant in the ground with your fingers while you pull the weed out.

Caging and Staking

These both sound like torture for plants, but they're not. They're ways of helping tall plants stand up straight.

Cages go around the outside of a plant. They're used for vegetables, not flowers, because they're not very pretty. Cages hold the stems up so the fruit doesn't lie on the ground and rot. They also keep big plants from spreading out too much.

You can buy cages that are 3 or 4 feet tall and wider at the top than at the bottom. They're fine for cucumbers, eggplants, and peppers. But even the biggest store-bought cage is too small around the bottom for tomatoes. A homemade cage is better.

With some help, you can make your own cages. The ones we made were about 18 inches across and 3 or 4 feet tall. They weren't tapered at the bottom, so they were stronger and held more than the ones you can buy. They were made of concrete-reinforcing wire, which you can buy from a lumberyard. You can also use strong fencing from a garden center. Make sure the spaces in the fencing are big, so you can stick your hand through and pick your food.

For homemade cages, you need to buy heavy 4-foot-tall stakes. Pound three of these into the ground around the plant and attach the cage to them with wire.

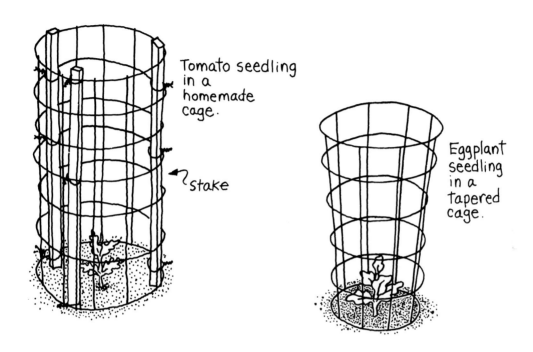

Tomato seedling in a homemade cage.

stake

Eggplant seedling in a tapered cage.

Staking is an almost invisible way to help flowers stay upright. Use one stake for each tall flower that makes only one or two stems. Push it into the ground next to the stem and tie some soft twine tightly to the stake. Now tie the twine loosely around the stem, so the twine holds it without squeezing it.

Some flowers, like tall snapdragons and zinnias, grow in big clusters. Don't try to stake each one. Put three or four stakes around the outside of the plant and wind a long piece of twine around the stakes. Don't tie the stems at all.

Usually you don't have to stake flowers until the buds form, but if they start to lean, stake them.

Staking tall flowers

wrap the twine around the stakes just below the flowers.

BUGS AND OTHER MUNCHERS

You never know who will visit your garden. We had toads, snakes, snails, insects, and birds. One day a snapping turtle laid her eggs next to the watermelons in the quickie compost pile. And once when we were trying to trap a woodchuck that had been lunching on some of our plants, we trapped a skunk instead. We managed to open the door of the trap and let it walk out, and nobody got perfumed. Later we found out that traps aren't a good idea. They aren't even legal in some states, because when the animal is moved to another animal's territory, there's usually a fight and one of them gets killed. A good fence may help keep animals out before they become a problem in your garden (see page 19).

The pests we had in the Kids' Victory Garden are problems for many gardeners: cutworms, cabbage root maggots, squash vine borers, Japanese beetles, cabbage worms, Mexican bean beetles, and of course the woodchuck. You may have different ones where you live. Your Cooperative Extension Service will be able to tell you what to expect. They'll also tell you what you can do about these pests without using chemicals.

We didn't use any chemicals to kill insects or animals. We just did our best to save our plants and otherwise shared the garden with the pests. They're much less dangerous than chemicals. By midsummer the pests had eaten some plants, but we had plenty of vegetables and flowers.

Most of your damage will probably come from insects. Here is a list of some of the big eaters, and some ideas for stopping them.

Opposite. *Gary and Ben with two garden visitors, one good, one bad. The worm will help loosen the soil, but the little round shapes are beetle grubs that grow up to be munchers.*

The Yardstick Garden

You don't have to worry much about pests. The outside fence will probably keep animals out. If you put cutworm collars on your peppers, they should be okay. If you have problems with Mexican bean beetles on your green beans, harvest the crop and pull the plants out. (You can eat the beans.) Then plant some more bean seeds. The plants could get hit by frost before they make any beans, but they might have time to give you a new crop.

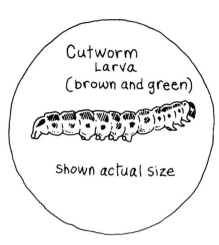

Cutworm
Larva
(brown and green)

shown actual size

Cutworms

You may never see the cutworms in your garden. They move along just under the surface of the soil at night, looking for tender stems. In the morning, all you see is a poor old broken plant lying on its side. Somewhere there's a happy cutworm.

Cutworms do most of their damage in the spring, to young seedlings. The best thing is to protect your seedlings with a cutworm collar as soon as you plant them. The cutworms bump into the collar and never get to the plant. You can buy cutworm collars in garden centers, but it is easy to make them out of paper cups by cutting the bottom half off. The collars should be about 4 inches tall. After you plant a seedling, slip the cup over the plant and push it about 1 inch into the soil. That's all there is to it.

Cutworms will eat some of the seedlings of plants you grow from seed too. But it's impossible to put little collars around every seedling. Don't bother. The cutworms probably won't eat the whole crop.

Sarah and Sam making cutworm collars out of drinking cups.

Good Guys

Don't get upset about everything that flies, crawls, jumps, and slithers into your garden. Some of these visitors are good for it, or at least not bad. At the Kids' Victory Garden we didn't worry about snakes or the snapping turtle. We were glad to see the worms, because they're good for the soil. And the toads and ladybugs were welcome because they eat bad bugs.

Honeybees are good for the garden too. They fly from plant to plant looking for nectar to make honey.

When they do this, pollen sticks to their legs. Pollen is the yellow, powdery, male part of a flower. As the bees fly around, the pollen from one plant lands on the pistil — the female part — of another plant. This is called pollination. Once a flower has been pollinated, it develops into a fruit.

Birds also pollinate plants. That's where the phrase "the birds and the bees" comes from. It's how plants make their seeds, and eventually their babies.

Cabbage Root Maggots

Cabbage root maggots are hungry little worms that grow up to be flies. The maggots come from eggs laid in the soil near a plant, which they think of as their local restaurant. The meals they like best are cabbage, broccoli, and cauliflower seedlings. We took care of the maggots by putting a maggot mat around each plant. This keeps the flies from laying their eggs close to the plants, so the maggots can't eat them.

You can sometimes find maggot mats in garden centers, but here's how to make them if you can't:

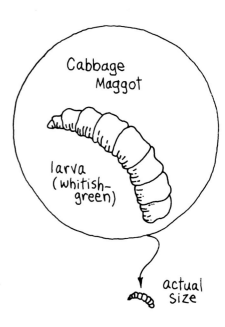

1 If you have them, use scraps of carpet, carpet underliner, or tarpaper, about 5 inches square. If you don't have them, use heavy cardboard.

2 With scissors, cut from the edge of the mat to the middle. Make a very small hole right in the middle of the square.

3 Slip the mat around the stem of the plant so it lies right on the ground.

4 Use waterproof tape to seal the scissor cut. If you made the middle hole too big and you can see soil around the stem, use the tape to close the hole too.

Maggot mats also can help take care of the cutworm problem, so you don't need a cutworm collar.

'Premium Crop' broccoli seedlings with maggot mats made of carpet underliner. We forgot the mats when we first planted, and lost two seedlings. Here, the mats are on and ready to be taped shut.

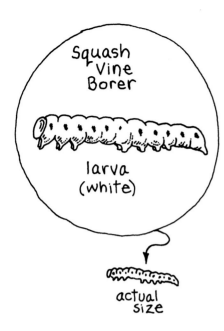

Squash
Vine
Borer

larva
(white)

actual
size

Squash Vine Borers

Squash vine borers are a big problem for most gardeners. They make holes in the stems of squash, melon, and cucumber plants, crawl inside, and start eating. You can't see them in the stems. The first thing you notice is wilted stems and leaves.

In the Victory Garden, Bob Thomson has had good luck by putting pieces of heavy aluminum foil, 15 to 18 inches square, around the base of each plant like a maggot mat. He does this for squash, zucchini, pumpkin, cantaloupe, and watermelon seedlings as soon as they're planted. (You don't need a cutworm collar.) For crops started from seed right in the garden, he puts the foil on when the plants are 4 or 5 inches tall.

If you are making foil reflectors for squash and pumpkins and other crops where two seedlings are planted together, just fold the foil where the two reflectors meet and tape it down.

The reflection off the foil seems to keep the borers away, at least for a time. The Victory Garden plants have survived longer with this technique than they ever did unprotected.

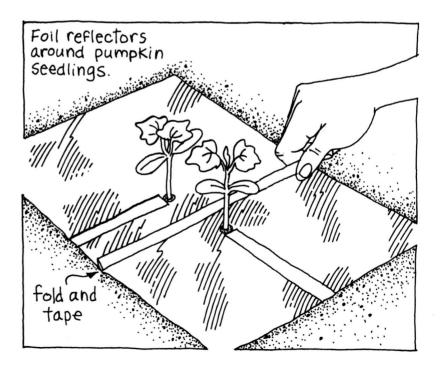

Foil reflectors
around pumpkin
seedlings.

fold and
tape

If the borers do come, there's one thing you can try, though it might not work. Look along the stem and find the hole where the borer went in. The borer may not be far away. Cut the stem lengthwise a little bit on both sides of the hole. If you find the borer, take it out.

We had borers in two zucchini plants. We did cut some out, and the plants made more zucchini. But there were probably other borers that we didn't get, and after a while both plants died. Luckily, we had a young zucchini plant growing, so we weren't out of zucchini for the summer.

Getting Eaten Alive?

It's not always easy to see the insects or animals that are eating your garden. You have to look for the damage they do.

Wilted plants.
This might mean that the plants need water. If water doesn't help, the wilting could be caused by an insect or a disease. (Plants do get sick sometimes.) If you can't take care of the problem, pull the plant out and throw it away.

Bitten leaves or fruit.
If the leaves are being eaten by an animal, you can see the bite marks working from the outside in. If insects are the problem, there will be holes all over the leaf.

Missing food.
This is usually caused by animals, mainly raccoons and woodchucks. If you live in the country, you may have deer. They're very hard to deal with, because they can jump over almost any fence.

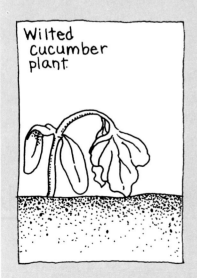
Wilted cucumber plant.

Bitten green bean leaves.

Woodchuck after tomato.

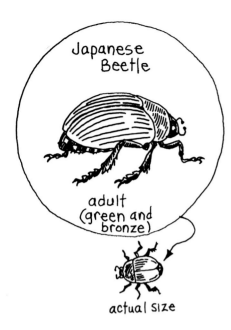

Japanese
Beetle

adult
(green and
bronze)

actual size

Japanese Beetles

Japanese beetles are shiny and copper-colored. They're pretty, if you like bugs. About seventy years ago a few of these beetles were hiding in plants that somebody brought from Japan, which is why they're called Japanese. Now they're everywhere — millions of them. They like zinnias, raspberries, grape leaves, and roses especially, but they eat most anything in the garden.

Without chemicals, there isn't much you can do about big numbers of Japanese beetles. But they're slow, so you can pick them off with your hands and drop them into soapy water to kill them. And you can put nets over some crops, like raspberry bushes. You'll still have some eaten leaves and vegetables. You'll have to live with it.

Joe peeling back the Japanese beetle netting so the other kids can harvest some raspberries from the bushes.

Cabbage Worms

These are green, and less than 1 inch long. If the leaves of your cabbage, broccoli, or cauliflower plants are being eaten, look on their undersides for these worms. You can try picking them off one by one, or you can hope you beat the worms to the harvest. If the leaves start looking really terrible, pull the plants out.

Mexican Bean Beetles

Mexican bean beetles first came to this country from Mexico. They are smaller than Japanese beetles, and they have dots on their backs. They like all kinds of beans. They went after the green bean plants in the Kids' Victory Garden. They left the leaves looking lacy, dotted with tiny holes. They don't eat the beans themselves, but if they eat enough of the leaves, the plants die anyway. When we saw that our bean plants were getting really chomped on, we harvested all the beans and pulled the plants out. That's what you should do, too.

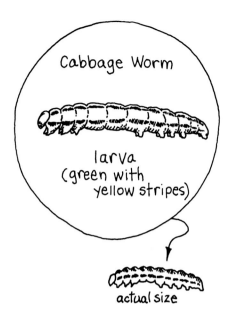

Cabbage Worm

larva
(green with yellow stripes)

actual size

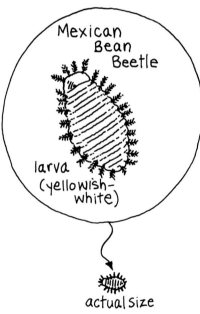

Mexican Bean Beetle

larva
(yellowish-white)

actual size

Mexican bean beetles chomping on the leaves of green beans. In one crop, all the plants' leaves were covered with these little porcupine-shaped insects.

Scarecrow

Scarecrows are supposed to keep birds out of the garden, because some birds eat seeds after you plant them. Luckily, scarecrows don't work too well, because birds also eat harmful bugs. We made our wonderful scarecrow just because it was fun.

A scarecrow should look sort of like a person. Ours had a head and hands, but if you don't want to be fancy, just make a cross so the scarecrow has a body and shoulders. (The shoulder piece is important. If you stick a broom handle in the ground and try to dress it, it will look like a broom handle with laundry hanging from it.) Adding a third piece of wood will give your scarecrow hips, so you can put pants on it.

Put the scarecrow in the garden where it won't shade your plants. Push it down into the soil as far as you can, so it stands up. Dress it any way you like. The clothes will be out there all summer, so don't use something anybody will want to wear again.

Shoulders

Nails

3'

2'

Hips (optional)

Nails

6'

Sarah, Julie, and Ben at work on the scarecrow. When it was finished, it stood up near the quickie compost pile.

HARVESTING

◄ Page 69. *Sam with an eggplant, just the right size for harvest.*

A harvest basket of eggplant, peppers, basil, and tomatoes, plus one pair of blue sneakers, ready for picking.

Finally it's time to eat the food. "Kids' Crops" gives you some special tips about picking different crops, but there are some general things to know too.

When Is It Ready?

Some crops, like onions, carrots, leeks, and potatoes, can be left in the ground even if they're ready to harvest. But most crops have to be harvested when they're ready. If you pick too early, the food may be hard or sour. If you wait too long, it might be bitter or tough.

Another big problem with harvesting too late is that the plant will stop producing so much. Plants make fruit so they can make seeds. If you harvest the fruit on time, the plant thinks it hasn't made seeds yet, so it keeps making fruit. But if you wait, the seeds are made. Then the plant thinks its job is done, and you get nothing more to eat.

The Yardstick Garden

The beans are ready when they're about this big:

The peppers are ready when they're this big:

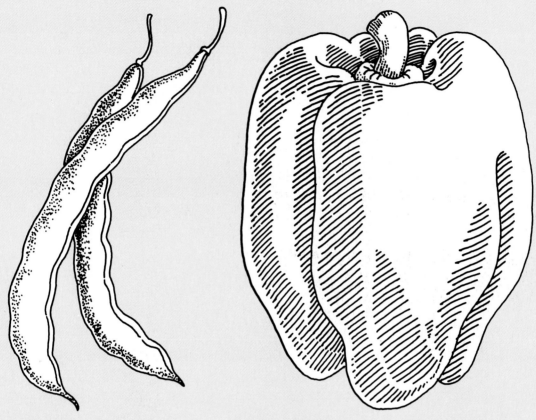

Pick all the beans that are ready and any that are too big. It's easy to miss some hiding under leaves, so look hard. When you pick, hold the plant with one hand and pull the bean off with the other. That way you won't pull the plant out. Be sure to pick beans every day, once they start coming.

You can pick hot peppers when they're green. Pick sweet peppers when they're green, or leave them to turn red. The red ones are sweeter.

Pick your zinnias whenever you want, with scissors so you don't crush the stem. (Get help with the scissors if you need it.) Take the flowers inside and put the stems in water. More zinnias will grow on the plant.

If a frost is coming, pick everything in your garden, because all the plants in the Yardstick Garden will die in the first frost.

Joe about to harvest a head of purple cabbage.

Picking the Harvest

Sometimes you can just use your hands to pick your crops. Other times you need scissors, or a knife, or a special strong pair of scissors called pruning shears. These are sharp, so get an adult's help if you need it. If you use a jack-knife, be especially careful to put the sharp edge of the blade against the plant. If you have it turned the other way, the knife can shut on your fingers.

Handling the Harvest

Fresh vegetables can't be thrown around, dropped from high places, or used for target practice. They're easily bruised. Set the vegetables down carefully. If you're picking different crops at one time, pick the heavy ones first so they're on the bottom of whatever you're using to carry them. (You can imagine what you get if you put a watermelon on top of tomatoes.)

The best container for your harvest is something that's wide at the top and holds its own shape. You can use a plain basket or a bowl or a cardboard box. Just put it down on the soil next to you and put what you pick into it.

Once we put Sam's share of a big midsummer harvest in a brown paper grocery bag. He wanted to carry it himself, but it was too big and heavy, so he had to bounce it along on the ground as he walked. By the time we got to the car, all the tomatoes had broken open. It was instant soup.

After Picking

Take the food inside right away. If you can't, keep it in the shade. When you're in the kitchen, separate the crops so all the eggplants are together, all the peppers are together, and so on. Wash them carefully in cold water, and make sure there are no bugs on them. Give them a chance to dry, then put them into plastic bags and place them in the refrigerator.

The harvest was divided every week. Sarah has potatoes, carrots, and green beans, and there's more to come.

Why Are Some Veggies Called Fruits?

If the part of the plant you eat is the part that contains the seeds, it's called the fruit. This means that tomatoes, eggplants, peppers, cucumbers, zucchini, and squash are really fruits, even though we usually call them vegetables and they're not sweet like sugar.

Not all vegetables are called fruits. It depends on what part of the plant you're eating. Potatoes, radishes, and carrots are not fruits, because you eat the roots. In the case of parsley, cabbage, and lettuce, you eat the leaves. And you eat the stems of leeks and chives.

A snack of garden vegetables and dip. (If you want to see the picture being taken, turn to page 145.)

Too Much Stuff!

One problem with gardening is that you may have too much good food at once. This happens mostly in August, and mostly with tomatoes and zucchini. It's hard to eat it all while it's fresh.

You can give some of your crops away, or make a big salad, vegetable soup, or spaghetti sauce. Or you can cut up raw vegetables and eat them with a dip. Carrots, broccoli, cauliflower, radishes, green beans, cucumbers, peppers, zucchini, and whole cherry tomatoes are all good this way. You can use blue cheese or Thousand Island salad dressing for a dip, or onion dip (made with sour cream and dried onion soup mix), or good ol' Russian dressing (ketchup and mayonnaise mixed). Or use anything you like.

CLOSING THE GARDEN

◀ Page 75. *Late in October, after the fall frost, when part of the garden has been put to bed. You can see the scarecrow's boots and the snapdragons along the fence, still flowering.*

After you work really hard, you need some good food and a rest. So does your garden at the end of the season. It needs to be fed and put to bed. This is the fall soil preparation. It isn't hard. All you do is add things and dig them in. It's like digging in the spring. There's no hurry, so you can take a few days.

Wait for the Fall Frost

The first frosts of the year usually happen at night. The next morning your warm-weather plants, especially the tomatoes, basil, green beans, squash, cucumbers, and zucchini, will be droopy. The leaves will wither and turn a dark color. Some plants won't die in the first frost. Lettuce, carrots, leeks, broccoli, cabbage, cauliflower, and parsley will all live until the weather gets colder.

After a fall frost, Julie, Ben, and Sam start the soil preparation in their little gardens. The zucchini plant in the front of the garden turned into a limp black mess in the frost, but the parsley plant next to it is still green and healthy.

This thermometer is reading at just frost temperature. If you notice that the temperature at sundown is around 40°F, you may have a frost during the night.

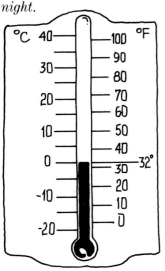

Clean Out the Garden

After the first frost, you can start to close the garden. Pull out the dead plants, roots and all, and add them to the compost pile. As the weather gets colder, all the plants will die, or at least stop making food or flowers. When this happens, pull them out. Don't pull out chive plants, because they're perennials and will grow again next year.

Take out all the tomato cages and stakes and save them for next year.

Test the Soil

The best time to do a soil test and fix the pH is in the fall. If you did a spring test and found out your lead level from a laboratory (see page 7), you can do the pH test yourself with a simple kit you can buy in a garden center. Or you can use a lab again.

You should do a soil test every year, because lime and sulfur wash out of the soil during the season. By fall every year, the pH of your soil will probably need fixing again.

To fix the pH, sprinkle lime or sulfur evenly over the garden. Call your Cooperative Extension Service to find out how much lime or sulfur to use.

Joe using a coffee can to sprinkle lime on a bed. Holding the can down near the soil helps keep the lime from blowing away.

The Yardstick Garden

Because the Yardstick Garden is in a corner of a bigger garden, it will be all taken care of in the fall. But you can help.

- When frost kills your plants, pull them out and put them on the compost pile.

- After the soil in the big garden is tested, sprinkle lime or sulfur over your garden to fix the pH.

- Rake up leaves or grass clippings from the lawn and throw them onto your garden. Add compost or manure, or both. Whatever organic matter is going on the big garden, put some on yours.

- Dig everything in with a spading fork. It won't be hard.

That's it for your Yardstick Garden. It's closed for the season.

Add Organic Matter

You've been adding organic matter all along. Now's the
time to add even more, starting with the oldest compost
you have. Then add the leaves you rake up in the fall, grass
clippings, and animal manure from cows, horses, sheep,
goats, chickens, or rabbits, but not dogs or cats.

It's best to have everything in small pieces, because
it will decay faster. If you see a big plant in your compost
pile, chop it up before you put it on the garden. You can put
whole leaves on the garden in the fall, but it's better if
they're broken up. We used a shredder, but you can go
back and forth over the leaves with a lawn mower and
shred them that way.

It doesn't matter in what order you put these things
on your garden. Just try to put 2 or 3 inches of organic matter on the soil every fall.

Dig In

Use your spading fork and turn the material in so it doesn't
blow away. When you're finished, use your spading fork or
iron rake to smooth out the soil and make it level.

Plant Winter Rye

Winter rye is like an extra blanket for your garden. It also
holds the soil in place through the winter. It's called "winter" because it grows even when it's cold. In the spring you
dig it in, and it adds even more organic matter to the soil.

You can buy little bags of winter rye seed at a garden center. Sprinkle the seeds on the soil and rake them a
little with your iron rake or spading fork. Then use the flat
part of the iron rake to pat the soil down and get the seeds
settled in the soil. When you're finished, water the seeds in.

John, Julie, Ben, Sam, and Joe throwing shredded leaves on the little gardens.

KIDS' CROPS

BASIL

A healthy plant of 'Sweet Basil' in midsummer.

This is a good crop because each plant is small, and you can eat the leaves all summer long. It's also one of the quickest plants you can put in your garden. If you start with seedlings, you will be picking leaves in about three weeks. The more leaves you pick, the more will grow.

Buying What You Need

The easiest thing is to buy seedlings in a cell-pack, but you can plant seeds in the garden. They grow quickly. A few plants will be plenty, unless your family really loves basil.

There are many kinds of basil. The most popular ones are 'Sweet Basil,' with green leaves, and 'Dark Opal,' with purple leaves. They taste about the same. They're both about 12 inches tall and about 12 inches across.

Planting
Don't plant basil until a week after your spring frost date, because it's very sensitive to frost. If you buy seedlings, put them in your garden 10 or 12 inches apart. Give each seedling a cutworm collar and make a fort of soil around it. Water them all with manure tea, fish emulsion, or water.

If you buy seeds, space them out in a furrow. Remember to keep them watered.

Taking Care of the Crop
If you plant seeds, thin the plants when they're about 2 inches tall. Leave one plant every 12 inches down the row. You can use the leaves of the little seedlings you pull.

During the summer, flowers will grow above the leaves. Cut the flowers off so the plant will keep making fresh new leaves.

Don't forget to water your crop, and pull weeds if you see them. And every two or three weeks, feed the plants with manure tea or fish emulsion.

Harvesting
You can start picking a few leaves when the plants are only 3 or 4 inches tall. Once the plant is full-grown, you can pick the biggest leaves every few days. You can even cut the whole top half of the plant off. As long as some leaves stay on the plant, it will keep making more.

Once the leaves have been picked, they will start to wilt right away, so don't pick them until you need them.

At the end of the season, when the fall frost is coming, pick the whole plant. You can then make up a big batch of spaghetti sauce or pesto. Or just take the leaves off the plants, put them in a plastic freezer container, and freeze them right away. You can use them all winter long.

How's It Taste?

Basil is an herb, which means it's used to flavor other foods. It's one of the tastes in spaghetti sauce. Sometimes it's called sweet basil, but it isn't really sweet. It tastes a little like licorice.

BEANS

Beans are easy to grow, and you get a big harvest from just a few plants. About two months after you plant, there are beans and beans and beans for two or three weeks. In the Kids' Victory Garden they were one of the big summer hits. The kids liked growing them, and they liked eating them raw while they worked in the garden.

Buying What You Need
You may be able to find bean seedlings, but beans are very easy to start from seed. The seeds are the bean-shaped things inside the green bean, so they're big and easy to plant. There will be many different kinds of bean seeds on the seed rack. The easiest ones are called bush snap beans. Make sure you see the words *bush* and *snap* on the package. We grew a variety called 'Greencrop.'

Planting
Beans will die in a frost, so don't plant them until a week after your spring frost date. Mark a path that is about 4 inches wide down the bed. It doesn't have to be very long, just 2 or 3 feet. Sprinkle the seeds on the soil about 2 inches apart, and poke each one into the soil with your finger, so they're 1 or 2 inches deep. Then close up the poke hole and pat the soil. When you're finished, water the seeds. Each seed will make one plant, which will make a lot of beans.

You can plant another crop about two weeks after the first one. That will mean green beans for most of the summer.

Taking Care of the Crop
There isn't much to do. Beans don't need to be thinned. When the plants are 2 or 3 inches tall, start feeding the crop with manure tea or fish emulsion every two or three weeks. And watch out for Mexican bean beetles, which eat the leaves until they look lacy (see page 67).

Aren't you cuke? where have you bean all my life?

Harvesting

The beans are ready to pick six or eight weeks after planting. Move the leaves and look for them. Sometimes they're hard to see. They should be 3 or 4 inches long, and as big around as your little finger. Don't let them get any bigger, or they'll be tough. When you pick the beans, hold the plant with one hand and pull the bean off with the other. Otherwise you might pull the plant out of the ground.

Once the beans start, they grow very fast. A little bean today might be ready to eat tomorrow. So look for beans every day.

If a frost is due, pick all your beans. They'll die if you leave them out.

BROCCOLI

At the Kids' Victory Garden, some kids thought they didn't like broccoli until they tried it raw with a dip. Ben likes his cooked, with a sauce made of sour cream, butter, lemon juice, and salt and pepper.

You can plant broccoli seedlings a week or two before your spring frost date, or wait until early summer. Some varieties grow one big head of broccoli and then little side heads for the rest of the summer.

Broccoli isn't good for a really small garden, because it's 18 inches wide, or wider, when it's grown. It also needs some special care. It's not one of the easiest plants in this book.

Buying What You Need

If you start with seeds, you wait a long time to pick the food. Seedlings are better. A cell-pack will give you all the plants you need. The variety we grew in our garden was called 'Premium Crop.' It's an All-America Winner, so it's a good variety for most of the country.

Broccoli, cabbage, and cauliflower are cousins. The seedlings look very much alike when they're young. If you buy more than one kind, keep the labels with them so they don't get mixed up.

Planting

Plant this crop where no broccoli, cabbage, or cauliflower has grown for the past four years. That's because a disease called club root can live in the soil for a long time and kill new seedlings.

Once you've found a place, put the plants in about 18 inches apart. If your soil pH is acid, mix a tablespoon of lime in the bottom of the planting hole to help prevent club root. Once the plants are in, give each one a drink of manure tea, fish emulsion, or water.

The big problem for broccoli plants is cabbage maggots. These insects will eat the plants, so you need to protect each plant with a maggot mat. (They're easy to make.

Sarah with a stalk of freshly picked broccoli.

See page 63.) Have the mats ready before you plant, so you can put them on right away. At the Kids' Victory Garden we waited too long to protect a couple of our plants, and maggots got them both. We had to pull them out.

Taking Care of the Crop

Broccoli plants don't need much attention during the season, other than the usual watering and weeding and a feeding of manure tea or fish emulsion every two or three weeks. But watch out for cabbage worms (see page 67).

Harvesting

After about two months in the garden, your big head of broccoli will be about 7 or 8 inches across. Harvest it right away. If you see little yellow flowers growing, you have waited too long. You'll need a knife to harvest, because you have to cut the stem below the head. You may need help.

The first side heads will be ready in a couple of weeks. They're just nibbles, but they're delicious.

CABBAGE

Cabbage can be a big plant, 18 inches across or more. Each plant makes one head of cabbage in the middle of the plant's big leaves. Cabbage is like broccoli and cauliflower. It's not a really easy crop, because you need to do some special things when you plant it so the bugs don't get it. It's not all *that* hard, though.

Buying What You Need

It's best to start with seedlings, because the seeds take so long to grow. If you buy a cell-pack, you'll have enough plants. They won't all be ready to harvest at once. You'll get one, and a few days later another one. The harvest goes on for about a month.

We put one crop in our garden in May. Then we went back to the garden center a month later and bought more seedlings. The harvest of the first crop was ending when the second one began. It's a good idea to plant two crops if you have the room and want a lot of cabbage.

When you're shopping, you'll find regular green cabbage and maybe varieties with purple leaves as well. They taste about the same, and you grow them the same way. The types marked 'Savoy' have crinkly leaves but the regular cabbage taste.

Planting

You can plant your cabbage right after you dig your garden in the spring. It won't be hurt by frost. Or you can wait until early summer. Cabbage is planted like broccoli. See page 86, and don't forget the maggot mats.

Taking Care of the Crop

If you've put maggot mats around your plants, they won't need much attention through the season. Just keep them watered and weeded, feed them every two or three weeks with manure tea or fish emulsion, and watch out for cabbage worms (see page 67).

Harvesting

The heads of cabbages are ready to pick when they're almost the size of a soccer ball. You can harvest them when they're smaller, but you won't get as much food from the plant.

You can leave cabbages on the plant for a little while after they're ready, but not for long. If they get too big, they split open. This can happen after a heavy rain, too. If the cabbage splits, harvest it and make some coleslaw.

You need a knife to pick cabbage. Get help if you need it. Just cut the stem right below the head. You can either pull the plants up and add them to the compost pile or leave them in the ground. Sometimes they make a few more small heads.

How far apart should your rows be? See page 38.

Sam's Gram's Coleslaw

Mix together:
6 cups shredded cabbage
¼ cup chopped scallions
¼ cup chopped carrot
Celery seed, if you like it

For the sauce, mix together:
1 cup mayonnaise
1 teaspoon salt
2 tablespoons sugar
2 tablespoons vinegar

Add the sauce to the cabbage a little at a time. There may be more sauce than you need. Put the coleslaw in the refrigerator for a couple of hours.

CANTALOUPE

To turn a pile of garbage into beautiful compost, see page 21.

Cantaloupes are melons, and they are a good crop for a great big garden or for a place off by themselves. One vine will grow to be about 6 feet long, or longer, and will make three or four cantaloupes about three months after the seedlings are planted. That's not much food from such a big plant, but the cantaloupes are so good they're worth it.

Buying What You Need
Planting seeds outdoors takes too long, so seedlings are best. Most garden centers sell them in peat pots so you can buy just the number of plants you want. Don't plant too many, even if you have a huge space. They all get ripe at once.

You can also start your own seedlings in peat pots, two or three weeks before your spring frost date.

Planting
Cantaloupes like warm weather. Don't plant them until a week or so after your spring frost date.

The first job is to find a place that's big enough. In our garden, we planted two seedlings on the quickie compost pile, along with the watermelons and pumpkins. All these plants need a lot of room. They also like warm soil and plenty of food. The compost pile has both.

Cantaloupes need a place that has 6 feet all around it. The plants will send out several vines this long. But one plant won't fill in all this space, so you can plant two seedlings 4 or 5 inches apart. They'll spread together.

When the seedlings are in, feed them with manure tea or fish emulsion. Then put an aluminum foil reflector around each one to keep the borers away.

Taking Care of the Crop
Cantaloupes don't need much attention. Just keep them watered, don't let the weeds take over, and feed them every two or three weeks with manure tea or fish emul-

sion. And look under the leaves now and then. The fruit hides under there.

It's time for a confession. We didn't get a single cantaloupe from the plants in the Kids' Victory Garden — just some tiny fruits that never got ripe. The problem might have been a squash vine borer that we didn't see. Or maybe there were just too many vines up there on that compost pile. Things like this happen to all gardeners. There are always surprises.

One moral of this story is that you have to keep your eyes open. Squash vine borers do love cantaloupe plants. If you see wilted leaves, borers may be at work. Page 65 tells how to dig them out.

Harvesting

Your cantaloupes are ready when the skin looks tan. Green skin means it's too early. If you're not sure, smell the fruit. Ripe cantaloupe smells ready to eat. When you pick, just push the stem off the fruit. If it doesn't come right off, the fruit's not ripe yet.

CARROTS

Sarah and a harvest of carrots.

Carrots don't take up much room, and they're easy to grow. The only problem is the tiny seeds, which are hard to space out when you plant them.

Buying What You Need

You have to buy seeds. There are lots of varieties to pick from. Some grow tiny carrots, and some grow big ones. The best ones for most gardens are the ones in the middle. They're supposed to be 6 or 7 inches long when they're full-grown, but sometimes they're smaller. 'Nantes Half Long' is the one we grew. Our biggest carrots were only 3 or 4 inches long. Maybe that's because we didn't thin them well enough. But they tasted fine.

If you want, you can order seed tape through a catalogue. The tape is easy to plant because the seeds are spaced for you.

Planting

Plant your carrots after your spring frost date or anytime until the middle of summer. Planting is easy, except for the tiny seeds. Rake the bed smooth and make a furrow with your finger. If you have a package of seeds, shake a few into your hand. Adding a little sand makes them easier to see and pick up (see page 37). Pinch a few seeds with your fingers and sprinkle them into the furrow. Each little seed becomes a carrot, so do your best to keep the seeds apart. After planting, gently close the furrow and water the row.

If you have seed tape, lay it in the furrow, cover it with soil, and water the row.

You can also scatter the seeds over a small area, maybe 1 foot square. Rake the soil first. When you scatter the seeds, try not to let them fall in a bunch in one place. Cover the area with a little soil and water it. The nice thing about this way of planting is that you probably won't have to thin the seedlings later. (But you may have more weeds.)

Taking Care of the Crop

When the tops of the carrots — the lacy green leaves — are about 2 or 3 inches tall, you have to thin them. Leave one seedling growing every 2 inches. You have to pull out most of the seedlings, but the ones you leave will do much better when they're not crowded.

As soon as you thin the row, start feeding the plants every two or three weeks with manure tea or fish emulsion (see page 52).

Harvesting

The root is the part you eat. About two months after you plant the seeds, pull one out and see whether it's big enough and orange all over. If it is, you can pull more. If not, wait a couple of weeks and try again.

You can pick a few carrots and leave the rest for later. You can even leave some in the ground for winter, if you cover them with a mulch before the ground freezes hard. See page 107 for help in doing this.

CAULIFLOWER

Sam with a head of cauliflower.
He picked the leaves off and
added them to the compost pile.

Cauliflower plants grow to be pretty big, about 18 inches across. You get one head of cauliflower to a plant, about two months after you plant the seedlings.

This is not one of the easiest plants to grow. It's related to broccoli and cabbage, so it needs some extra care when you plant it. The extra care takes time, but it's not hard.

Oh, petunia, you're what I cauliflower.

Buying What You Need
There are two kinds of cauliflower. One is regular white cauliflower. The other is purple, and looks and tastes like a cross between cauliflower and broccoli. We grew the white kind, which is the one you see most in garden centers, in our victory garden.

Seeds take a long time. Seedlings are quicker. In the Kids' Victory Garden we planted both. That gave us two crops, and a lot of cauliflower. You'll probably have all you want by growing seedlings.

Planting
Cauliflower doesn't do well in a frost, so plant after your spring frost date. Otherwise grow it like broccoli and cabbage. See page 86 for directions, and be sure to make the maggot mats before you start.

Taking Care of the Crop
You don't have to do too much. Just keep the plants watered and weeded, feed them every two or three weeks with manure tea or fish emulsion, and watch for cabbage worms.

Harvesting
Cauliflower is ready about two months after you plant it. The heads will be at least the size of a big grapefruit (probably bigger), and a pale yellow-white.

The vegetable that you eat is a bunch of flower buds. If you leave the head on the plant for an extra day or two, it starts to flower and doesn't taste as good. So pick cauliflower as soon as it's ready. Cut the stem just under the head. The stem is very tough and hard to cut. You'll need a knife, and maybe some help.

CHIVES

Chives are an herb. That means they're a flavoring for foods like baked potatoes and salads. They're not usually eaten alone, but the kids at our garden liked to munch on them fresh.

Chives look like tall grass and taste like mild onions. Like onions, they make bulbs underground. You might notice these when you look at the roots. They are small and white. Chives are easy to grow, and they make beautiful lavender flowers that you can pick for drying. Chives are a perennial, so they come up every spring, bigger than the year before.

Buying What You Need

You don't need more than one plant. Usually they're sold in little pots rather than in cell-packs. You can buy these as soon as your soil is dug and plant them in the ground right away. Frost doesn't hurt them.

Planting

Perennials stay in the ground a long time, so most people like to plant them in a corner of the garden. You can do your soil preparation in the fall without having to work around the chives. You might want to put them near the kitchen so you can pick them for salad. You can also put them in a big pot for the summer, then move the pot indoors for the winter.

Because chives stay in the ground for a long time, dig in some extra compost or old manure when you plant them. Each plant needs a space that's about 12 inches all around. Water them in with manure tea, fish emulsion, or water.

Taking Care of the Crop

Chives are really easy. All you should do is feed them once a month or so with manure tea or fish emulsion and keep them watered and weeded.

Chives grow flowers in the spring. You can pick some, but make sure you pick the stem right down at the base of the plant so you don't leave broken stems to rot. If you don't pick flowers for a bouquet, wait for them all to die, then cut the whole plant off, almost to the soil. It'll send up new chives in no time.

Harvesting

You can pick chives anytime you want. When you do, cut a whole long stem; don't just chop off the top. You can pick a few at a time or a whole handful.

After fall frost, when you put the garden to bed, cut the green stems off 2 inches above the soil. In the spring the roots will send up new chives.

> **Before you plant anything, the soil should be soft enough to dig with your hands. See page 14.**

CUCUMBERS

**What's the spring frost date in your area?
See page 9.**

Cucumbers are easy to plant and easy to take care of. They like warm weather, so they're a good crop if you don't start your garden until after school. One problem with them is that they can get sick, which makes them wilt and sometimes kills them. They're still worth a try.

Buying What You Need

One or two plants will give you a few cukes at a time all summer long. Cucumber seeds are big and easy to plant, so you can start with seeds. Or you can buy seedlings.

It doesn't matter which variety you buy. Most grow on big vines, but some grow on bushes, and they're a little bit smaller. Some varieties are called burpless, which means they don't make you burp. And some varieties are pickling cukes. These cucumbers are small, and tasty even if you don't use them to make pickles.

Planting

Don't plant your cukes until a week or more after your spring frost date. They don't like the cold at all.

Cucumbers take up a lot of room. You can put them in a big spot and just let them go, or plant them either along the back fence of your garden or in a cage. In the Kids' Victory Garden we grew both vine and bush cucumbers in 4-foot cages. You can buy the cages in a garden center, or you can make them if you have some help (see page 58). The cage holds the plant in so it doesn't take up so much space.

If you're going to use a homemade cage, put two seedlings about 12 inches apart in the row. The cage will fit around them both. If you use tapered cages, put one plant in a cage. If you're planting more cucumbers, the cages should be 3 feet apart. After planting the seedlings, put a cutworm collar around each one and give the plants a drink of manure tea, fish emulsion, or water.

If you're planting seeds, put two seeds about 12 inches apart. Three feet away, put another two seeds 12 inches apart. Water the seeds after you put them in the ground.

Taking Care of the Crop

When the plants are about 10 inches tall, put one cage around each pair. While they grow, keep them watered, and don't let the weeds take over. Feed them with manure tea or fish emulsion every two or three weeks.

If the leaves start to wilt, the plants are probably sick. Pull them out and throw them away. The disease might be living in the soil, so don't plant any more cukes in that spot for a year or so.

Harvesting

The cucumbers are ready about two months after planting, when they look like cucumbers. If they stay on the vine too long, they get too big and bitter. Keep looking at your vines every day, because cucumbers grow fast. Pick up the leaves and look hard. Some might be hiding.

When you harvest, hold the cucumber and twist it off the stem. You can eat the skin of homegrown cucumbers. They're tender, and they haven't been waxed like grocery store cukes have been.

DAFFODILS AND OTHER BULBS

chionodoxa

scilla

When you're closing your garden in the fall, you can plant some flowers to come up next spring. You can't plant every kind of flower in the fall. But if the flower grows from a bulb or something like a bulb and it's sold in the fall, you can plant it.

Daffodils and tulips and hyacinths are big bulbs and make big flowers. Crocuses, scillas, and chionodoxas are small bulbs and make small flowers. Daffodils, crocuses, scillas, and chionodoxas are especially easy for kids because they grow new flowers every year. (Tulips and hyacinths may flower for only a year or two.)

Buying What You Need

Buy any bulbs you like. You can shop at a garden center, starting in September, or you can order bulbs by catalogue. The seed houses send out special bulb catalogues in the fall, with pictures that will help you decide what to buy.

One daffodil bulb often makes two or three flowers, but most other bulbs make one flower. They look pretty if you plant a few together, so buy at least three of each kind of bulb you want.

Buy some bone meal, too, at the garden center. This is ground-up animal bones, which makes good bulb food. Buy the smallest bag you can find.

Planting

Plant your bulbs in September or October, so they have some time to grow a little before the ground freezes hard. The easiest thing is to close the garden and then plant a few bulbs in the corners or along the edges.

Before you start to plant, sprinkle some bone meal on the bed and dig it in to give the bulbs some extra food. Then set all the bulbs on the bed, in the places where you want them to come up. Put the tall ones behind the short ones. The bulbs shouldn't touch each other, but they can be

close together. That makes the flowers come up close together, which looks nice.

Now just plant the bulbs, one at a time, right where they're sitting. Big bulbs have to be planted 6 or 8 inches deep. A trowel makes a good hole for tulips and daffodils. Put one bulb in the bottom of the hole, with the tip pointing up. The tip is the pointy end. Some bulbs don't have much of a point, but you can usually tell which end is really flat, and that's the bottom. When the bulb is planted, fill the hole with soil and then press it down.

Little bulbs don't have to be so deep. If your soil is soft, you can just push the little bulbs down with your hands so the tips are covered with 3 or 4 inches of soil.

After the bulbs are planted, water the bed well.

Taking Care of the Crop

The flowers will come up in the spring. They fade after a couple of weeks, but the leaves stay green for a long time. Then they turn brown and die. While the leaves still have some green, the bulbs draw strength from them for next year, so you have to let the leaves die on the plant. Don't cut them off until they're brown.

Harvesting

You can pick the flowers if you want. Use scissors and cut them so the stem is nice and long.

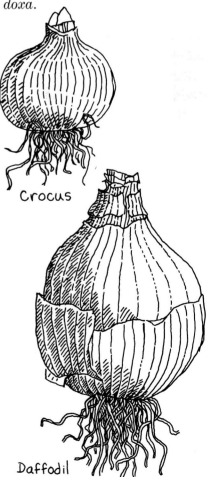

Yellow daffodils in bloom. The little purple flower is a chionodoxa.

Crocus

Daffodil

EGGPLANTS

Sam and Jenny with a harvest basket, and a perfect eggplant.

These are not plants that make eggs. But in most varieties, the eggplants are shaped sort of like a big egg with very dark purplish skin. The inside is white and tastes very mild.

The plants don't get too big, and each one makes three or four eggplants late in the summer. The plants grow slowly, and sometimes they get sick. But they're easy to plant, and usually you get enough eggplants anyway, so they're a good crop.

Buying What You Need

Start with seedlings, not seeds. Our variety was 'Dusky,' which is good where summers are pretty short. One or two plants is plenty. One fruit is probably enough for a family meal.

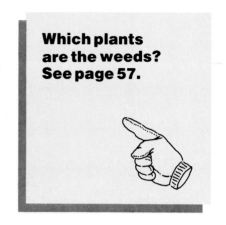

Which plants are the weeds? See page 57.

Planting

Wait until a week after your spring frost date, because eggplants can't handle a frost. Then plant the seedlings 2 feet apart. Give each seedling a cutworm collar and make a fort of soil around the outside of the collar. Water them with manure tea, fish emulsion, or water.

The eggplant fruits are a little heavy, and sometimes they fall off the plant. So we put a small cage around each plant in the Kids' Victory Garden. This kept the plants from spreading very much and helped to hold the fruit up. You don't have to use cages, though.

We put our eggplants and peppers in the same row. They do well together because they're about the same size. They're also planted at about the same time and harvested at about the same time.

Taking Care of the Crop

Make sure the whole garden is watered, especially in hot weather. Pull weeds if you see them. And feed the plants every two or three weeks with manure tea or fish emulsion. There's nothing much to do if they have a disease except pull them out and throw them away.

Harvesting

Eggplants are ready about two months after you put in the seedlings. The skin should be shiny. You can pick eggplants when they're about 4 inches long, or wait and let them get a little bigger. Sometimes the really big ones are tough and seedy, so try to pick them before they get longer than 6 or 7 inches.

IMPATIENS

Two pots of impatiens, in a flat with lettuce seedlings.

Impatiens plants are covered with flowers all summer long. They're really easy to grow, and they're one of the few flowers you can put in a shady spot. The colors are white and different shades of pink and red. Some of the colors are very bright and some are pale. The plants are small enough for a small garden.

Buying What You Need

You won't have any trouble finding impatiens plants, and that's what you should buy. Don't bother with seeds. For the Kids' Victory Garden, we bought two full-grown plants, one white and one a bright orange-red. We left them in the pots and put them outside under a tree.

Impatiens also come in cell-packs, if you want more than one or two plants. If you buy a variety that's a mix, you'll probably get different flower colors, but they're usually pretty together.

Planting

If you want to put your plants in your garden, take them out of their pots and space them 12 inches apart. They don't need a cutworm collar, but they do need a fort of soil to hold water. After they're planted, give them some manure tea or fish emulsion.

You can also put three impatiens plants together in a big hanging pot. Or space them about 10 inches apart in a window box. That's closer together than impatiens are usually planted, but it's okay.

Make sure you don't plant your impatiens until a week after your spring frost date.

Taking Care of the Crop

Keep impatiens watered. That's the important thing, especially if they're growing in pots or a window box, where they'll dry out faster. Check them every day during hot weather. If the soil seems dry, water them. And if you see the plants droop, water them right away. If the leaves look yellow, give the plants another dose of manure tea or fish emulsion.

Harvesting

There's no harvest with impatiens. The stems aren't strong enough to make a bouquet. Just enjoy them while they flower. They'll die in the first frost, and you can put the plants on the compost pile.

Names and Nicknames

All plants have real names, called botanical names. Some have nicknames too. The botanical name of impatiens is *Impatiens*. The nickname is "Patient Lucy." Look for either one when you shop.

LEEKS

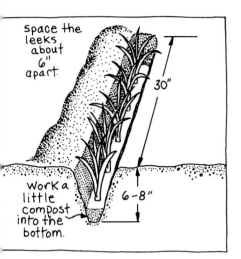

space the leeks about 6" apart

30"

6-8"

Work a little compost into the bottom.

Leeks look like giant scallions and taste like mild onions. You have to do a little extra digging when you plant them, but they're still pretty easy. And they don't mind the cold. They can even stay in the garden over winter, if you cover them.

Buying What You Need

Look for seedlings at the garden center. This is a crop that probably won't come in a cell-pack. Most garden centers sell them in flats, which have many plants in them. Buy the seedlings early in the season, because the longer they sit in the flats, the more tangled the roots get.

If you can't find seedlings, plant seeds. You can order seed tape through a catalogue, or you can buy a package of seeds. There aren't many varieties to choose from.

Planting

Plant leeks as soon as your soil is ready in the spring. They take a long time to grow, so don't wait until summer.

The first thing to do is to dig a trench — a ditch with a flat bottom. It should be 6 to 8 inches deep and 4 inches across. A hoe will make a good trench. To grow six leeks, you need a trench about 30 inches long. Put some compost on the bottom and dig it in a little.

To plant seedlings, make poke holes 6 inches apart in the bottom of the trench and put the white roots in the holes. The roots should be covered, and the green leaves should stand straight up and down. When you're finished, give all the seedlings some manure tea, fish emulsion, or water.

To plant seeds in the ground, make a furrow in the bottom of the trench. Space the seeds out in the furrow and cover them with soil. Make sure you water them.

Taking Care of the Crop

If you plant seeds, thin the row when the seedlings are about 3 inches tall. Leave one plant every 6 inches.

Feed the plants every two or three weeks with manure tea, fish emulsion, or water. And every week or so, fill in the trench with about 1 inch of soil at a time. Just pull some soil in from the side. Don't bury the plants. Make sure the tips always show and are standing straight. By early summer the trench should be completely filled in.

Harvesting

Begin your harvest in the fall. You can pick leeks earlier, but they won't be very big. If you leave them in the ground a long time, they'll be okay.

When you harvest, dig the leeks out with a shovel or spading fork. The roots will come too. You can cut these off.

In the Kids' Victory Garden we harvested some leeks in the fall and covered the rest with mulch to keep the soil from freezing hard. One day in February we went out in the snow and dug them up. They were a little frozen, because the winter had been bitterly cold. But they were great.

Mulching for Winter

One good winter mulch for leeks is the leaves that you rake up in your yard. It doesn't matter what kind of leaves you use, as long as they're dry. (You can also use hay or straw.) Pile the mulch up high and loose, so you cover the plants. The deeper the mulch, the better. Put a big sheet of plastic over it to keep it dry. Hold the plastic down with rocks or pieces of wood or plastic bags full of leaves.

In the winter you can peel back the plastic, move the leaves, and dig out fresh vegetables. You can take a few and cover the rest for later.

LETTUCE

Here's a great plant for a kid's garden. It's really easy, not very big, and grows quickly. It's happiest in cool weather, but you can usually keep lettuce going all summer if you buy varieties that can take the heat.

Buying What You Need

Lettuce is so popular that you'll find different varieties of seedlings with no trouble. Some, like 'Iceberg,' make tight heads. Most have loose leaves. Sometimes the leaves are dark green, sometimes almost red. We grew six different varieties, all of them delicious. 'Mission' is a good variety in hot weather. We didn't grow 'Iceberg' because it does well in only a few places in the country.

See what your garden center has, and buy healthy seedlings of a variety that looks good. Don't buy more than one cell-pack at a time. They'll all be ready to eat at once. If you want lettuce all season, buy and plant a new cell-pack every couple of weeks.

You can also plant seeds out in the garden. This is a good idea late in the spring, when you may have trouble finding seedlings. The seeds are small but pretty easy to handle. Just plant a few seeds at a time, so you don't have too much lettuce at once.

Planting

If you're planting seedlings, put them in the ground about 12 inches apart. They don't need cutworm collars, but do make a fort of soil around each one, and give them a drink of manure tea, fish emulsion, or water.

If you buy seeds, make a furrow in the soil. Sprinkle a few seeds down the furrow, spaced out the best you can. Or drop three or four seeds every 12 inches down the furrow. This will make thinning easier. When the seeds are in, close the furrow and water the seeds well.

Lettuce run away together.

Oh, no. We cantaloupe.

Taking Care of the Crop

If you plant seeds, thin the seedlings when they are about 3 inches tall. There should be one seedling every 12 inches. And make sure you keep the garden watered. Lettuce wilts easily if it starts to dry out. Once every two or three weeks, feed the plants with manure tea or fish emulsion.

Harvesting

Start your harvest when the plants are 8 or 10 inches across. You can pick the outer leaves and leave the rest to keep growing, or harvest the whole plant by cutting it off with a knife. It's important not to let lettuce stay in the garden once it's ready to pick.

Three varieties of lettuce. The 'Ruby' is the red-leafed, 'Salad Bowl' is light green, and 'Oak Leaf' is dark green.

MARIGOLDS

Ben buying marigold seedlings at the garden center.

Marigolds are easy, colorful flowers from Mexico, where they grow wild. Mexico is hot and sunny, and that's the kind of weather the plants like best when they grow in a garden too. They'll flower all summer if they get enough sun.

Buying What You Need

There are dozens of different marigolds. One good choice is called 'Nugget.' These plants grow to about 10 inches tall and start making flowers as soon as you plant them. There are gold, orange, brown/red, and yellow 'Nuggets,' and mixed colors too.

If you can't find 'Nugget' seedlings, buy another variety that won't get taller than about 12 inches. If you buy taller ones, you'll have to stake them so they stand up straight (see page 58).

Planting

Wait until after your spring frost date to plant marigolds. You can put them anywhere — in a row in the garden or along the outside edge, or in a window box or a big pot. They should be spaced about 8 inches apart. Make a fort of soil around each seedling, and give them all some manure tea or fish emulsion.

Taking Care of the Crop

You have to keep the plants watered, especially if they're in pots or window boxes, where they'll dry out very fast. Give them some manure tea or fish emulsion if the leaves look yellow. If you want to keep the plants looking their best, pick off old flowers when you see them.

Harvesting

You can pick a few flowers for a little bouquet if you want. Or just leave the flowers on the plants.

Don't plant your seedling too deep. See page 47.

ONIONS

Ben and his mother planting onion sets. The flowers behind them are phlox.

Onions are one of the easiest crops you can grow in your victory garden. You can harvest them early as slim green scallions, or wait and pick big round onions.

Buying What You Need

You can find seeds and seedlings, but it's better to buy a bag of little onions called onion sets. They're faster than seeds or seedlings, and a cinch to plant. You'll find sets for yellow and white onions in garden centers early in the spring.

Planting

The important thing is to plant early, as soon as your soil is ready. If you wait until your spring frost date to plant, the plants won't have enough time to make big round onions. You can harvest young onions, though, called scallions.

Planting onion sets is as easy as pie. Lay them on the soil, tips up, about 4 inches apart down a row, and push them into the ground so the tips just show. (If your soil isn't soft enough to push them in, dig it some more.) Water them, and you're finished.

If you plant the sets 2 inches apart instead of 4, you can harvest every other one for scallions and leave the rest to become big onions.

Taking Care of the Crop

Keep the onions watered with the rest of the garden. And don't let the weeds take over. Every two or three weeks, feed the crop with manure tea or fish emulsion.

Harvesting

If you want scallions, they're ready when the green stems are about 6 inches tall. Just pull them out.

If you want small, young onions, harvest anytime. If you want onions that you can keep for a long time, harvest them three or four months after planting, when the stems are brown and lying flat on the ground. They'll come right out when you pull them.

Don't forget to fix the pH before you start your garden. See page 17.

PARSLEY

Did you finish the digging?

Only parsley.

Parsley is an herb that is used all the time in cooking. The kids at our victory garden liked to pick it and eat it raw. It doesn't get very big, and you can start to harvest when the plant is very young. Parsley lives a long time, right up until the ground freezes.

Buying What You Need
Buy seedlings of either curly parsley or the kind with flat leaves, which is sometimes called Italian parsley. You will probably be able to find a cell-pack, or bigger plants in pots.

Planting
It doesn't matter when you plant parsley. You can do it as soon as your garden is dug or wait until summer. Parsley plants are usually easy to find.

Put the plants in the garden, 12 inches apart. Make a fort of soil around each one, and water them with manure tea, fish emulsion, or water.

Taking Care of the Crop
Just keep the plants watered, pull weeds nearby, and feed them every two or three weeks with manure tea or fish emulsion.

Harvesting
You can start picking sprigs — each sprig is one stem of parsley, with all its leaves — when the plants are 6 or 8 inches across. Break or cut the stem near the soil, not right under the leaves where there would be broken stems left to rot. Don't harvest all the leaves at once during the season. Leave a few on the plant so it can keep making new ones.

In the late fall, when the ground is starting to freeze, harvest all the parsley. In the kitchen, cut the leaves from the stems, put them in a freezer container, and freeze them. They'll be tastier than dried parsley.

Julie cutting yellow leaves off her parsley seedlings before planting.

PEAS

Do chives give you hives?

No, but peas make me sneeze.

These were one of the favorites in the Kids' Victory Garden. Fresh peas are so sweet they're almost like green candy. And they're easy to grow. All they need is something to climb on and cool weather. Peas are one of the first crops you can plant in your garden.

Buying What You Need

Buy seeds. Shop carefully so you get the kind of peas you want. If you want to eat the peas themselves, buy regular green peas. If you like pea pods, like the ones in Chinese cooking, buy edible-podded peas.

If you can't make up your mind, or if you want to eat some as peas and some as pods, buy snap peas. 'Sugar Snap' is a very good variety if you have a good strong fence, 5 or 6 feet tall, for them to climb on. If your garden fence is only 3 feet tall, try one of the shorter varieties, like 'Sugar Ann' or 'Sugar Daddy.'

Planting

Plant your peas as soon as the ground is ready. At the latest, get the seeds in the ground two or three weeks before your last spring frost date. They just can't face the summer.

Peas are easy to plant. The peas are the seeds, so they're big and easy to hold. They'll sprout a little faster if you soak them for two hours in warm water before you plant them. You don't have to do this, though.

Plant a path of pea seeds about 4 inches wide in the soil right in front of the fence, if you have one. Just drop the seeds on the soil so they don't touch. Poke each one in with your finger, fill in the hole with soil, and water the seeds. That's it. You'll see sprouts in a week or two.

If you don't have a fence, push some dry twigs into the ground right where the seeds are. The twigs should be

as tall as the plants will get, and have several branches but no leaves. As the plants grow, they'll climb up the twigs.

If you start early enough in the spring, you can plant another crop two weeks after the first one and have a longer harvest.

Taking Care of the Crop

Peas don't need thinning. Just keep them moist, don't let the weeds invade them, and feed them every two or three weeks with manure tea or fish emulsion.

While they grow, make sure all the vines are holding onto the fence. They use their tendrils, which are like green threads that wrap right around the fence wire, to do this. If you see a vine leaning out, gently weave the top of it through the fence. The tendrils will do the rest.

Harvesting

The peas are ready in about two months. If they're regular green peas, the pods will be about 3 inches long. You'll be able to see the little peas inside the pod. You should pick the pods when the peas are smaller than the frozen peas you can buy in a store.

If you are growing edible-podded peas, pick the pods while they're still flat, with only tiny peas inside. Don't let the peas get too big.

You can pick snap peas when the peas are still tiny, and eat the pods. Or leave them until the peas inside grow. They get sweeter as the peas develop, and they're good as long as the pod is bright green, even if it seems ready to burst.

The Fresher the Better

Before you pick your peas, set the table and get the cooking water hot. Cook them instantly, because once they're off the vine, they start to lose sweetness right away. That's why the ones you grow are so much better than the ones you buy.

PEPPERS

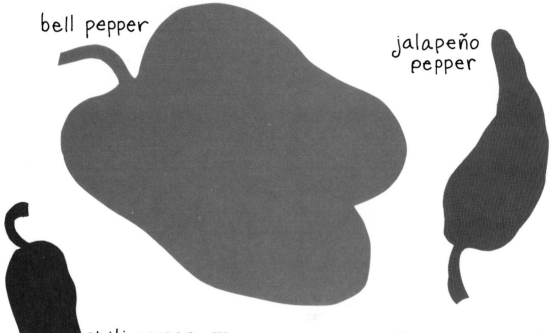

bell pepper

jalapeño pepper

chili pepper

We grew sweet peppers and hot peppers in our victory garden. Some of the kids had never had a hot pepper, so we tasted them when we harvested. One kid really liked them a lot, and one kid really didn't. They feel like they are burning your mouth.

Pepper plants are medium-size. You can grow them even in a small garden. They start making fruit about two months after you plant seedlings, and the harvest keeps going all summer.

Buying What You Need

Buy seedlings in a cell-pack. If you have the space, you can plant them all. Make sure you know whether you're buying hot peppers or sweet ones.

'Gypsy' is a yellow sweet pepper that was a big hit in the Kids' Victory Garden. It's an All-America Winner that produces between one and two dozen fruits through the summer. 'Bell Boy Hybrid' is another All-America Winner. The fruit is green at first, then red. One 'Bell Boy' plant won't make as many peppers as 'Gypsy,' but the peppers will be great.

Planting

Peppers need warm weather, so wait until a week after your spring frost date to plant. Then put the seedlings in the ground 18 inches apart. Put a cutworm collar around each seedling, and make a fort of soil around each one. Give them a drink of manure tea, fish emulsion, or water.

Taking Care of the Crop

In the Kids' Victory Garden we put peppers in small cages. This kept them from spreading and helped the plants hold up their fruit. If you want to try this, put the cages on within about two weeks of planting. If you wait, the plants will be too big for the cages. (For more about cages, see page 58.)

Peppers don't need much care once they're in the ground. Just make sure they're watered, weeded, and fed every two or three weeks with manure tea or fish emulsion.

Harvesting

Start your harvest two months or so after you put your plants in. You can pick sweet peppers when they're green and about the size of an apple. Depending on the variety, it might be a big apple or a small one. If you leave them on the plant, they'll turn red and be much sweeter.

Hot peppers come in different shapes and sizes, so there's no rule for when they're ready. You can harvest peppers at any size. You can pick a few when they're small and leave others to grow.

Hot and Sweet

When you are buying hot peppers, look for words like *chili*, *jalapeño*, *cayenne*, or just plain *hot*. If you want sweet peppers, look for *banana*, *bell*, or *sweet*.

Sometimes vegetables are really fruits. See page 73.

PETUNIAS

Don't forget to get your soil tested for lead. It's a poison. See page 8.

Petunias come in almost every color you can think of. The plants stay small, but they're really flowery if they grow in full sun. If they have too much shade, the stems get too tall and floppy.

Buying What You Need

Buy seedlings in the color you like. Look for nice short seedlings, no taller than 3 inches. If you can't find any, buy the shortest, fullest plants you can. Then pinch or cut the tops off so they're 3 or 4 inches tall. When they grow, they'll fill in and make more branches.

You'll probably find about a hundred different kinds of petunias. You'll see words like *standard*, *single*, *double*, *multiflora*, and *grandiflora*, which describe the size of the flowers. It doesn't really matter what you buy, but the multifloras are a good choice. The flowers are not too big, and there are lots of them.

Planting

You can plant petunias a little before your spring frost date, but they'll do better if you wait until after frost. If you put them in the garden, space them about 12 inches apart. Make a fort of soil around each one and then water the seedlings well with manure tea or fish emulsion.

Petunias can be squeezed a little in a window box, to 9- or 10-inch spacing. And you don't need the fort of soil.

Taking Care of the Crop

Keep the plants watered. When the flowers fade, pick them off so the plants look neater. If the leaves start to look yellow, give the plants some manure tea or fish emulsion.

Harvesting

Petunias aren't good flowers for a bouquet. Just leave them in the garden until you're ready to close it for the winter. They'll still be making a few flowers, even when it's pretty cold.

John looking over the cell-packs of white petunias at the garden center.

POTATOES

A wheelbarrow with a fresh harvest of potatoes and carrots.

Potatoes take a little digging, but they're not hard to grow and you get quite a few potatoes from a 3-foot row. They're ready to eat in about three months, but you can sneak a few before that.

What to Buy

Buy a small bag of seed potatoes. You'll probably have more than you need. (For a 10-foot row, you'll need about a dozen.) Most garden centers have all-purpose potatoes, like 'Superior' or 'Kenebec.' All-purpose means you can bake or boil them. If you only like baked potatoes, look for a Russet or Idaho variety. Some garden centers also sell potatoes with red skins, like 'Red Pontiac' and 'Norland.' These are delicious boiled or made into potato salad.

Planting

Plant your potatoes after your spring frost date. Start by digging a place to plant them. In our victory garden, we just used a hoe and dug a little V-shaped ditch 5 or 6 inches deep.

Planting potatoes is a breeze. Just drop in a whole seed potato every 9 to 12 inches. Potatoes have spots on them called eyes. The stems grow from the eyes, so at least one eye should point up to the sky. Fill in the ditch with soil, pat it down a little, and water the bed. You'll see stems coming up in a week or two.

Taking Care of the Crop

Every two weeks or so, pull some soil around the bottom of the plants to make a mound and bury the potatoes a little deeper. Give them some manure tea or water every two or three weeks, too. This will help the leaves grow, which helps the potatoes grow.

Harvesting

After two or three months, the plants' leaves and stems will start to die. When they are completely withered, the potatoes are ready. Pull the stems out and put them on the compost pile. Then use your hands to dig down through the soil. You can use a spading fork instead, but you might stab a few potatoes. Make sure you find every one. They might be 8 or 10 inches away from the seed potato, so search hard.

When you're finished, leave the potatoes on top of the soil for an hour or so. This will help them dry out a little. Then you can take them into the house. Don't leave them out too long, or the potatoes will get too dry.

New Potatoes

You can harvest a few baby potatoes before the crop is really ready. Watch for the plants to flower. Two weeks later, pull the soil away with your hands and feel for the potatoes. Take no more than two or three, about the size of an egg, from each plant. Cover the rest with soil and leave them to grow to full size.

PUMPKINS

Pumpkins, one carved for Halloween, with yellow gourds, which are squashes grown for decoration, not eating.

If you have a big garden or a separate place where the pumpkin plants can roam around, this is a good crop. Pumpkins need a long time in the ground, but they aren't much trouble. One plant will make only three or four pumpkins, so don't expect too much.

Buying What You Need

The best variety for you depends on what you want and how much space you have. Most pumpkins grow on vines, which get to be 6 or 8 feet long. 'Spirit' is a good variety. Some other varieties have vines that are 15 feet long. There are also some varieties that grow on short vines, almost like a bush. They are a little bit smaller, but still big plants. 'Cinderella' is a good bush variety.

If you want to grow pumpkins for pie, look for a sugar pumpkin, like 'Small Sugar.' If you want a well-shaped Halloween pumpkin, try 'Jack-O'-Lantern.'

If you can find seedlings in the variety you want, buy them. Otherwise buy seeds. We started our crop from seed right in the garden at the end of May, and had our first harvest at the end of September. You can also start the seeds indoors, two or three weeks before your spring frost date. Put one seed in each peat pot.

Planting

Wait until a week after your spring frost date and then find a planting site that has at least 6 feet all around it. We planted our pumpkins on our quickie compost pile, and they still went a little wild. One vine snuck into the garden and climbed a cucumber cage. Then a pumpkin grew inside the wire of the cage, and we couldn't get it out.

All varieties are planted in the same way. Draw a little circle in the soil, about the size of a saucer. If you have seedlings, plant two across from each other on the circle. Water them with manure tea, fish emulsion, or water. To keep squash vine borers away from the plants, try an aluminum-foil reflector (see page 64).

If you bought seeds, put two or three around the circle and poke them in with your finger. Cover them with soil and water them well.

Taking Care of the Crop

If you've planted three seeds to a circle, wait until the plants are 2 or 3 inches tall and cut off the smallest one. When they're 4 or 5 inches tall, you can put aluminum foil reflectors around them.

If your pumpkins are outside the garden, don't forget to water them. And watch for wilted leaves. It might mean squash vine borers, which are trouble. See page 64 for more details.

Harvesting

Pick pumpkins when they turn orange. It usually takes all season for this to happen. Use pruning shears to cut the stems about 3 inches from the fruit. Don't yank the stem off, or your pumpkin won't last very long.

Pumpkin plants will die in the first frost, so harvest and bring them inside if the weather is supposed to turn cold.

How to Grow a Whopper

Some people have grown pumpkins that weigh 600 pounds and are as big as a small car. Without chemical fertilizers, you can't grow one this big, but you can still grow a doozy. First you should buy the right variety. The official World Pumpkin Confederation suggests 'Atlantic Giant.'

Start the seeds in pots about three weeks before your spring frost date. Plant the seedlings in the garden after your spring frost date, and put some extra compost in the soil. Give them some manure tea or fish emulsion every week or so. When the pumpkins are as big as softballs, snap off all but the two biggest. If new pumpkins grow, take them off so the plant will put all its energy into the two you saved. Then stand back and figure out what you're going to do with pumpkins that weigh more than your parents. Good luck.

Dad   Mom   Pumpkin

RADISHES

Radishes are the quickest vegetable you can grow. You can eat them only three or four weeks after planting. You've probably tasted them. They're usually red on the outside and white on the inside, and hot all over. All varieties are milder if they grow in cool weather.

Radishes are quick and easy, but they don't always work. Bugs get after them sometimes, and all you get are little red strings instead of radishes. They're still worth a try.

Buying What You Need

You have to buy seeds. 'Cherry Belle' is an All-America Winner. We grew 'Crimson Giant' in the Kids' Victory Garden. If you want regular red radishes instead of white ones, look at the picture on the package and make sure that's what you have.

Planting

Plant early in the spring if you don't want your radishes to set your mouth on fire. We planted ours in the middle of May and got a good crop.

   To plant, make a furrow and drop the seeds in, spaced out the best you can. The seeds are small, but they're round and easy to handle. Each seed becomes one radish, so a row that's 1 foot long will give you twelve radishes, if the bugs don't get them first. Close the furrow and water the row when you finish.

Taking Care of the Crop

About ten days after planting, thin the seedlings so they're 1 inch apart. Keep the crop watered and weeded, too. About two weeks after planting, feed the radishes with manure tea or fish emulsion.

Harvesting

The radishes are ready in about a month. You can't really tell by looking, though you might be able to see the top of the radish itself, which is the root. If you think they're ready, pull one up and see. If one is, they all will be soon.

You might need some special gardening tools for kids. See page 10.

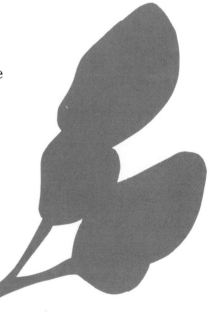

SNAPDRAGONS

White, orange, yellow, and pink snapdragons. The short pink flowers with dark leaves are wax begonias, another good flower for a kid's garden.

These flowers are great for bouquets and easy to grow. They do best in the spring, when the weather's cool. Most of the other flowers in this book like summer best, so snapdragons are a good choice if you get an early start in your garden.

Buying What You Need

Buy seedlings. Most varieties are mixed colors, so you'll have some white, red, yellow, and pink ones in a cell-pack. Some varieties are 3 or 4 feet tall, some about 20 inches, and some less than a foot. We had the best luck with the middle-size ones. They made a few flowers all summer long.

Planting

One plant will make several stems and several flowers, so you need to give snapdragons some room. Put the tallest varieties about 1 foot apart, the middle-size ones about 10 inches apart, and the little ones 6 or 8 inches apart. Make a fort of soil around each one, and give them all some water.

The really tall varieties will probably need staking. Page 58 tells you how to do this.

Taking Care of the Crop

Snapdragons bloom most in early summer. When they start making fewer flowers, you can cut the flower heads off to help the plants make new flowers. If the leaves turn yellow, give the plants some manure tea or fish emulsion.

Harvesting

Pick snapdragons anytime you want. Cut them far enough below the flowers so they have a stem you can put in water.

Snapdragons

These flowers are called snapdragons because if you squeeze the flower, it opens and looks like a dragon's mouth, or so somebody thought once. Some varieties make a snapping sound when you squeeze them.

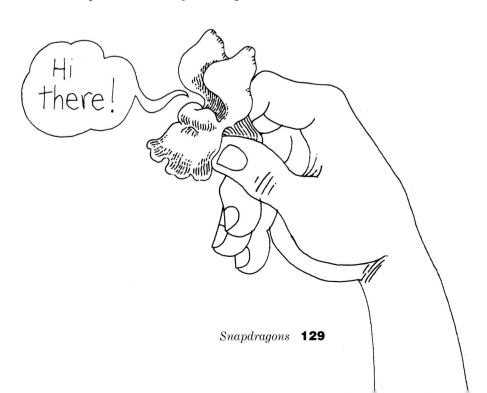

SQUASH

Butternut
Squash

Squash plants are related to pumpkins, watermelons, and cantaloupes. But squash and pumpkin plants are stronger than melons, and you'll probably have good luck with them. Squash plants are usually vines that can grow 6 or 8 feet, even 15 feet, long. The bush varieties don't sprawl so much, but they're still huge. All varieties take a long time to grow.

Buying What You Need

There are many different kinds of squashes. Hard squashes, like butternut, acorn, and Hubbard, are called winter squash, because they are harvested in the fall and can be stored for winter. (If you want to grow summer squash, look up zucchini, on page 140.)

Acorn
Squash

Blue Hubbard
Squash

Spaghetti
Squash

We liked the vine variety 'Waltham Butternut' best. The squash is wonderful, and the plants seem to be able to fight off squash vine borers. 'Bush Acorn Table King' is another good variety, and smaller than some other squash plants. It's about 3 feet across when it's full-grown. 'Jersey Golden Acorn' is a great All-America Winner, and fairly small, too.

If you can't find seedlings, you can start with seeds.

Some bugs are good bugs. See page 62.

Planting

Even though they're called winter squash, these plants don't like cold weather. Don't put them in until a week after your spring frost date.

Find a place with at least 6 feet all around it, where the plants can stretch out. At your planting place, draw a circle in the soil about the size of a saucer. If you're planting seedlings, plant two across from each other on the circle. Water with manure tea, fish emulsion, or water. Aluminum foil reflectors will help keep the borers away and are easy to make (see page 64).

If you are planting seeds, put two or three around the circle, poke them in, and give them a good drink of water. You won't need to thin the seeds.

Taking Care of the Crop

You don't need to do much to squash. Keep the plants watered and feed them every two or three weeks with manure tea or fish emulsion. When the plants are 4 or 5 inches tall, you can put the aluminum-foil reflectors around them.

Harvesting

The squashes are ripe in the fall, when their skins are really hard. A butternut squash is ready when the skin is beige, with no green lines on it. Use pruning shears to cut the tough stem, and leave a stump of the stem on the fruit so it stays fresh as long as possible.

SUNFLOWERS

Gary standing next to full-grown sunflowers. (Ben took the picture.)

Most varieties of sunflowers produce enormous plants and enormous flowers that look like giant black-eyed Susans. They're easy to grow, and you can harvest the seeds in the fall. Even though they're so tall, they're skinny, and they don't need much space. We had some borers in our plants, and the squirrels went after them too. But we still had flowers.

Buying What You Need

In the Kids' Victory Garden we grew the variety 'Mammoth,' which is the biggest you can buy. The plants grow to be 10 or 12 feet tall. The flower has a huge "face," where the seeds are, and some yellow petals that look like hair. They're not exactly pretty, because the flowers are so big that they hang down over the stem. But they are amazing. In the big varieties, one seed makes one flower.

Buy seedlings if you can. We couldn't find any, so we planted seeds at the end of May, and had flowers around Labor Day. The flowers start out small and keep growing.

Planting

Wait until after your spring frost date, then find a place for the sunflowers where they won't shade the rest of your garden. We put ours next to the big fenceposts on the north side of the garden so we could stake the stems to the fenceposts.

When we planted, we put three or four seeds around the base of each fencepost, about 4 inches apart. If you want them to grow as big as they can, they need more room. Plant two seeds about 2 inches apart every 12 inches down a row.

Remember to water the seeds after you plant them.

Taking Care of the Crop

If you plant seeds in a row, you need to thin so there's only one seedling every 12 inches. We didn't thin our fencepost sunflowers at all. Give the plants some manure tea or fish emulsion if you see yellow leaves.

When the stems are about 3 feet tall, tie them to a stake so they'll grow straight. Tie a string tightly around the stake and then loosely around the plant.

You'll have to stake the plants once or twice again as they grow. Put the last string right up under the flower so the stem doesn't bend over. You'll need a ladder, and some help.

Harvesting

Most people don't want a bouquet of sunflowers, but if you do, go ahead and pick the flowers when they're fresh.

For the Birds

You can harvest the heads of your sunflowers and use them for birdseed. After the petals fade and drop off the plant, cut the flower heads off, leaving about a foot of the stem attached. Put them in a dry place where mice won't get them. When the stem is crisp, tie it to the branch of a tree. The birds will come and eat the seeds. Or you can rub your hand over the face of the flower to make the seeds fall out, and put the seeds in your birdfeeder.

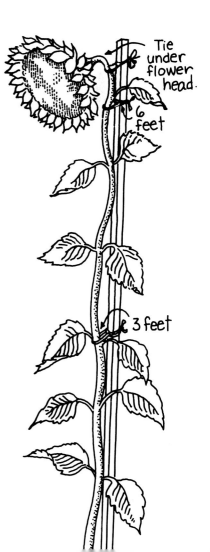

Tie under flower head.

6 feet

3 feet

TOMATOES

regular tomato

cherry tomato

plum tomato

There's nothing as good as a home-grown tomato. Some gardeners don't grow anything else. They're easy, except the plants are big and floppy, so you need to help them stand up.

Tomatoes aren't a really quick crop. You'll wait two months after planting for your first tomato. But the harvest is huge, even from one plant. And the tomatoes keep coming until frost.

Buying What You Need

Buy seedlings. You'll find so many different ones, you might not know what to buy. You need to know that there are three main kinds of tomatoes: regular tomatoes, cherry tomatoes, and plum tomatoes.

Regular tomatoes are the size of an apple. You can eat them fresh or use them for cooking. Good varieties are 'Big Girl,' 'Better Boy,' 'Celebrity,' and 'Champion.'

Cherry tomatoes are small. You can't do much cooking with them, but they're great fresh.

Italian plum tomatoes are long and slim and better cooked than fresh. They're the best ones for spaghetti sauce.

You can buy cell-packs, but one plant makes a lot of tomatoes and takes up a lot of space. So if your garden center has single tomato plants in pots, you might want to buy just one or two. One cherry tomato plant and one regular tomato plant are probably plenty.

Planting

Wait until a week after your spring frost date and dig some extra compost or old manure into the soil where the tomatoes are going. Then plant the seedlings 3 feet apart. Put a cutworm collar around each one. Make a fort of soil around the collar, and give each plant a drink of manure tea, fish emulsion, or water.

If your seedlings are tall and scraggly, you can plant them so some of the stem is underground. You shouldn't do that with most plants, but you can with tomatoes.

You can put a cage around each plant after you put them into the ground. If you buy the tapered cages at a garden center, buy the 4-foot size. We found that these weren't big enough around the bottom, so we used some homemade cages that were about 18 inches across, top and bottom, and 3 or 4 feet tall. They did a better job of holding up the plants. For more about cages, see page 58.

If you don't want to make cages, you can tie your tomato plant to a strong wooden stake that's 6 feet tall. Tie the twine tightly around the stake and loosely around the plant's stem.

Taking Care of the Crop

Except for the regular watering and weeding, the only thing you need to do is feed the plants. In the Kids' Victory Garden we put some old manure on the soil around the plants two or three weeks after planting. Every time it rained, the plants got another drink of manure tea. Tomatoes need extra food. If you want, you can feed them with manure tea or fish emulsion every two or three weeks through the season instead.

Harvesting

Wait until the tomatoes are red all over, with no green around the top. That means they're really ripe. Then just pick the fruit. Don't squeeze it, or the skin will break. Check your plants every day, and pick what's ripe. If you leave tomatoes on the plant, they get too ripe and fall off.

One for a Pot

If you want a small plant you can grow in a pot, try 'Pixie.' It's about 15 inches tall when it's grown. The tomatoes are almost full-size.

WATERMELON

To be really happy, watermelon plants want a long season, warm weather, and a big space to crawl around in. We did our best, and we got some fruit. They weren't great, but watermelons are fun to try anyway, if you have a big garden.

Buying What You Need

Buy seedlings. If you can't find them and you live in the North, don't bother growing watermelons. They won't have enough time to grow if you plant seeds in the garden. (You could start your own seedlings, though, two or three weeks before your spring frost date.)

Most varieties grow vines that spread along the ground and get to be 6 or 8 feet long. Bush varieties are a little bit smaller, but still huge. Bob Thomson has had good luck in the Victory Garden with 'Sugar Baby,' a small variety of watermelon.

Watermelon seedlings are usually sold in peat pots, one plant to a pot. One or two plants is plenty.

Planting

Wait until a week after your spring frost date. If you have a long summer, wait longer so the soil and air are really warm. In the North we have a short season, so we need to plant as soon as we can after frost.

Plant one watermelon seedling in a spot with at least 6 feet all around it. You can put a second seedling in the same site, about 3 inches away. Your planting place should be far from other crops, or the vines will climb all over everything.

If the seedlings are in peat pots, plant the pots too (see page 46). When the plants are in the ground, water them with manure tea, fish emulsion, or water. Then, to help scare off the borers, try an aluminum foil reflector around the plants (see page 64).

Sarah doing her best with a very slippery watermelon.

Taking Care of the Crop

There isn't much you have to do. Keep the plants watered and weeded. Watch out for squash vine borers. And hope for good weather.

Harvesting

Some people say that if you knock on a ripe watermelon, it sounds full instead of hollow. The truth is, it's hard to know when a watermelon is ripe. If you live in the North, leave the fruit on the plant as long as you can, even though it won't grow too much in the fall. Harvest it if a frost is due, or it will die. When you harvest, use a knife or pruning shears to cut the fruit from the vine.

ZINNIAS

John picking zinnias with pruning shears, so the stems don't get crushed.

These flowers come in all different sizes and colors, and they're all easy. Some are only a few inches tall, and some are 3 feet tall. The flowers of some varieties are really big. They all bloom for most of the summer, and you can pick them for a bouquet.

Want a scarecrow in your garden? See page 68.

Buying What You Need

Buy seedlings. The important thing is to buy the color and size you want. If you don't want to stake your flowers, buy a variety that won't get more than 2 feet tall. The 'Peter Pan' zinnias come in a lot of colors and grow to be about 1 foot tall, so they don't need staking.

How to Plant

Wait until a week after your spring frost date. Then you can put your zinnias right in your garden. Put the 'Peter Pan' zinnias about 12 inches apart and the tall ones about 18 inches apart. Make a fort of soil around each plant and fill the fort with manure tea or fish emulsion.

Taking Care of the Crop

Keep zinnias watered and weeded, and feed them with manure tea or fish emulsion if the leaves turn yellow. If you plant a tall variety, it will need staking around the outside of the plant. See page 58 for more details.

Harvesting

You can pick zinnias anytime you want. It's a good idea to pick all the flowers, so the plants will keep making more.

Bugs

Japanese beetles love zinnias. There isn't much you can do about this, except pick the beetles off. They probably won't ruin the whole crop. (For more about these bugs, see page 66.)

ZUCCHINI

*Joe with a freshly picked
perfect zucchini*

Zucchini plants are big, but they're a good crop for kids.
They make a lot of food, and even if you don't like green
vegetables, zucchini don't have a taste to be afraid of.
They're very mild and a little bit crunchy.

Buying What You Need

Seedlings are fastest and easiest. There probably won't be
much choice, so buy what the garden center has. You can
buy seeds too. They're big and easy to plant. Either way,
don't grow too many plants. Just one will give you so many
zucchini you'll be standing on street corners giving them
away.

Zucchini is a kind of summer squash. It's different from winter squash, which you harvest in the fall and can keep until winter. If you want regular green zucchini, make sure that's what you buy. There are other kinds of summer squash too.

Planting

Zucchini plants need a big space. When they are full-grown, they're 3 or 4 feet across and 2 feet high, with huge leaves. We put two plants up on the main compost pile in the back of the garden, where they had plenty of room.

To plant zucchini seedlings, put them in the ground 3 feet apart, and add a scoop of compost to the hole if you can. If you put them in a row, make sure it's a wide row. Water them with manure tea, fish emulsion, or water. If you want to keep the borers away, make an aluminum foil reflector for each plant (see page 64).

If you plant seeds, put two or three together, not touching, in a spot that's 4 feet across. In the Kids' Victory Garden we put in two seedlings a week after our frost date, and two or three weeks later we planted another crop from seed right in the garden. This turned out to be a good idea, because the first crop was hit by borers just as the second crop was ready to harvest.

Taking Care of the Crop

If you plant seeds, thin the crop so there's only one plant growing in a 4-foot space. As they grow, keep the zucchini watered and weeded. And feed them every two or three weeks with manure tea or fish emulsion.

Harvesting

When the zucchini fruits are 6 or 8 inches long, they're ready. To pick one, just hold it and twist it off the stem, or cut the stem, which is a little safer for the fruit. Pick up the leaves and look hard to make sure you get all the ripe ones. If you miss one, it'll grow so big you can use it for a baseball bat. When a plant makes one giant zucchini, it doesn't make as many tasty little ones.

FOR PARENTS AND TEACHERS

John introducing Ben and his brother Christopher to a garden visitor. The older kids and younger kids worked wonderfully together.

Adults were always on hand in the Kids' Victory Garden. I was there every day, along with Gary Mottau, who did so many things for the garden and this book. He took the pictures and got all the tools and materials ready for the garden every morning. The kids came to the garden only once a week, so Gary kept an eye on the garden between sessions. He watered it, and sometimes did emergency weeding and harvesting.

Other adults were there too. Bob Thomson spent some time with us and talked about the garden's progress. Nancy Lattanzio came from WGBH, the station that produces *The Victory Garden* for public television. She helped Gary with film and cameras and held reflectors on days when the sun was so bright that the kids' faces were in shadow as they worked.

And Julia McConnell also came on most days; she's a college student who played with the younger kids if they felt like leaving the garden for a while. Sometimes they played in Ben's big sandbox, and sometimes they raced around the yard together, whooping it up, or hung out next door on Bridget's swing set. They'd play for a little while, then wander back into the garden to do some more weeding or to check on the progress of the pumpkins.

The garden was set up in two parts. In one big section, which we called the main garden, we worked together and planted different vegetables and flowers. Then we divided a smaller section into seven little gardens, so that each kid had a garden in which he or she could choose the crops and plant and take care of them.

This was a good combination for learning and experimenting. The kids wanted to know the right way to do things, but they also wanted a place to play with what they had learned. The play was different for each kid. Joe stood in his garden with a hoe, weeding in careful short strokes, while Ben dug up and moved his chives almost weekly.

We met every week for about two hours. At the beginning of each session we worked together in the main garden. Later the kids went off on their own, to play or work wherever they wanted. At the end of every session we all shared the harvest. Even with so many people around, there was always plenty for everybody.

About halfway through each session we'd have a rest and a snack. We tried to make snacks of things that come from the garden — if not ours, then someone else's. We might have a bowl of strawberries and raspberries that we picked ourselves, or juice and zucchini muffins, or cut-up vegetables and dip. Once we made ice cream, but we didn't have enough time to let it get fully hard, so we ended up with delicious raspberry milkshakes.

All along, Gary and I looked for ways to keep things simple. We didn't let the hard work go on for too long. Every fifteen minutes or so we moved on to a new task. If the kids wanted to wander off, we let them. We wanted them to like what they were doing. We also wanted them to learn enough about gardening to have good harvests. Kids, like adults, like to succeed at what they're doing.

We tried to pass on a respect for nature's way of doing things. For this reason, and for safety as well, we didn't use any chemical fertilizers, pesticides, or fungicides in the garden. We didn't think kids should be around chemicals, and we had a great garden without them.

The kids learned so much, and they learned fast. Within a few weeks they knew about cell-packs and trowels and compost. They knew what different plants looked like while they were growing. They learned how to reach into a zucchini plant and harvest the fruit, and how to tell a really ripe tomato

from an almost ripe one.

All the kids, no matter how old, could do real things in the garden, with real results. Even the youngest kids tried everything, and did a good job, with some help. The older kids helped the young ones, and they all enjoyed the different jobs of gardening — even weeding — if the tasks were done in small doses.

And the kids liked what all gardeners like about gardening: good food. Each kid had a favorite crop. For Julie it was parsley. For Sam, cauliflower. Everybody loved the tomatoes and green beans. ("I liked chives!" Sarah said at the end of the summer. "For a while they were my favorite vegetable!") There was always a lot of eating during harvesting. The kids would snap open the peas and munch on a few while they picked. Or they'd wash off carrots and eat them then and there. Or they'd pick a tomato, warm from the sun, and eat it like an apple.

The Victory Garden Kids' Book is for kids of all ages. Kids older than nine or ten will probably be able to read the book and follow it on their own, if somebody is nearby to answer questions and help out. Joe and Jenny and John were almost adults in terms of what they could do in the garden. They had energy and concentration and could finish the jobs they

Some of the little gardens as they looked midseason. They weren't neat, but the kids did them all on their own, and they produced some good crops.

started. By the time we disbanded in the fall, they really were seasoned young gardeners.

Kids younger than seven or eight are young enough to feel that a garden is magic. Sam and Ben and Sarah and Julie brought a level of energy and enthusiasm to the garden that surprised us all. Of course young kids need more supervision. They're apt to water only half a row of seeds, or yank out seedlings they think are weeds. That's fine; these are normal mistakes. The adults just need to be sure that the mistakes don't ruin a crop and disappoint the hopeful kids.

As the adult in the kids' garden, your job is to help when it's needed and to do some cheerleading. You don't have to be a gardener yourself. All the information you or the

Gary photographing the kids during a snack, with Nancy holding a reflector to improve the light. (So much for kids not liking vegetables, by the way.)

kids need is in this book. You can learn together. If you are an experienced gardener, communicate enthusiasm and pleasure and loosen up on your standards for logic and order. Kids care if their plants die, but they don't care about maximizing space or keeping the garden tidy.

Above all, it's important that the kids see the garden as theirs rather than yours — that they have a good time, get their hands down in the earth, appreciate the wonder of watching plants grow and make flowers and food, and know that they have a part in it all. In the complicated world our kids live in, these are real gifts.

INDEX